SATANIC STRATEGIES

Fred DeRuvo

Satanic Strategies

Copyright © 2010 by Study-Grow-Know

All rights reserved. Written permission must be secured from the publisher to use or reproduce any part of this book, except brief quotations in critical reviews or articles.

Published in Scotts Valley, California, by Study-Grow-Know
www.studygrowknow.com • www.adroitpublications.com

Scripture quotations unless otherwise noted, are from The Holy Bible, King James Version. This version is in the public domain.

Images used in this publication (unless otherwise noted) are from clipartconnection.com and used with permission, ©2007 JUPITERIMAGES, and its licensors. All rights reserved.

Any Woodcuts used herein are in the Public Domain and free of copyright.

All Figure illustrations used in this book were created by the author and protected under copyright laws, © 2010, unless otherwise noted.

Additional research and assistance: Marie Swanson

Cover Design and Interior Layout: Fred DeRuvo

Cover Image: Loup-Garou © *David Espin*

Library of Congress Cataloging-in-Publication Data

DeRuvo, Fred, 1957 –

ISBN 0982644361
EAN-13 9780982644362

1. Religion – Demonology & Satanism

CONTENTS

Foreword: 5

    Chapter 1: The Truth: It's Out There 7

    Chapter 2: Tares and Wheat: The Ever-Widening Gap 38

    Chapter 3: The Delusion: Believing the Lie 46

    Chapter 4: Satanism: The Illuminati and Freemasonry 57

    Chapter 5: Satanism: Entertainment 66

    Chapter 6: Satanism: Satanic Ritual Abuse SRA 124

    Chapter 7: Satanism: Pedophilia 143

    Chapter 8: Satanism: Sexual Perversion 160

    Chapter 9: Satanism: Serial Killers 168

    Chapter 10: Satanism: New Age Movement 175

    Chapter 11: Satanism: Drugs & Human Trafficking 181

    Chapter 12: Satanism: Mind Control 225

    Chapter 13: Satanism: Islam, Jihad, and Sharia 231

Satanism: More to Come 240

for your sakes forgave I it in the person of Christ; Lest Satan should get an advantage of us: for we are not ignorant of his (strategies).

– 2 Corinthians 2:10b-11 (KJV)

FOREWORD

I was not intending to write another book that deals with the spiritual realm of demons, that is, until I received a few emails from a woman named Marie Swanson. Marie shared how much she appreciated my books and then told me a bit about her background. It was interesting to realize how much God has used this woman to thwart the powers of darkness. By thwarting I mean she *exposed* them and their works, just as we are exhorted to do in Scripture (cf. Ephesians 5:11).

In the course of her adult life, she has seen much, experienced much, and helped much. Some of the things she has previously been involved in are wrong (and she is the first to admit it). Nonetheless, the insight she gained from those experiences gave her a firsthand understanding of how Satan works. They provided her with a clearer comprehension of the deceptions he frequently employs to accomplish his purposes.

Unbeknownst to Marie, the Lord seemed to be piquing my interest in some of the same areas. Even though I have published two books previously on the subject, there was more to write. One of the books I was reading at the time was by Brannon Howse titled, *Grave Influences: 21 Radicals and Their Worldviews That Rule America from the Grave.* A fascinating book that puts together in one package the histories of many of the individuals that, by themselves may not have accomplished much, but as Satan used them (under God's watchful eye), connecting one to the other, it became very clear that an extremely diabolical scheme has been in the making for quite some time.

The reality is that Howse's book forced me to consider anew the reality of the spiritual realm, and Satan as the prince of the power of the air. Though fully defeated, he obviously retains power and ability, which he uses in his attempts to thwart God's plans and create a world in which he is the ruler, not God. It was about that time that Marie wrote asking if I had ever heard of "Walk-ins." I could not say I had, so I modified my search to include that area.

This then led to other areas of research in the demonic realm, in which Satan's minions take on every form of masquerade in order to deceive. It boggles the mind when considering just how massive and complex in scope the level of deception foisted upon humanity. Too many individuals are completely unaware of Satan's subterfuge tactics and go blissfully along believing that what they experience must be correct due to their spiritual bliss. If not corrected, they will unfortunately find that what they thought was bliss, was nothing more than a front, with hideously raw evil lurking just beyond reach and out of sight.

This book was written simply because it needs to be. With Marie's permission, tremendous research, and blessing, I have used a great deal of information she has gathered in her years of research. That coupled with my own research provides an in-depth picture of how Satan has worked to destroy God's original design. It is my prayer that her information will reveal the true sense of evil that is growing exponentially throughout the world today. I pray that if you are caught up in it, you will see it for what it is and do everything you can to run from it, by calling on the Name of Jesus Christ!

God is here to help. He loves you and He wants you free from the tyranny of Satan's lies, deceit, and overall grip. I pray that you will see the truth that is only found in Jesus Christ and embrace it. May God be with you and bless you.

Fred DeRuvo, June 2010

SATANISM
The Truth is Out There

In the 1970s and 80s, there was what has become known as the Satanic Ritual Abuse scare or panic. People like Mike Warnke, Lauren Stratford, and Rebecca Brown published books about their own journey through the darkly evil halls of Satanism. They spoke of ritual sacrifices, abuse, and other things for which satanic worship became known.

Within a very short time, people like Bob and Gretchen Passantino published articles and books that attempted to debunk these and other individuals. They were successful, because soon, Warnke was discredited, along with Stratford and Brown. The tone of articles by the Passantinos first published in Cornerstone magazine was uncharitable to say the least. It seemed as if they actually came out of the gate with both guns blazing. In short order, Stratford's credibility was shot along with her reputation and the folks at Cornerstone were patting themselves on the back for a job well done, having believed that they had saved the public from further alleged defrauding by these people.

Did Cornerstone Magazine *gain* anything? It would seem so. They gained increased subscribership, greater credibility, and became one of the go-to groups for the final word on Satanism and cults, at least on the west coast. Certainly, with additional subscribers came a wider audience. With a wider audience came additional money.

The Passantinos went on to write their own book on Satanism. The book is 96 pages, and is broken up into eight chapters. The authors spend time highlighting the history of Satanism all the way up to and including the modern period. It seems that they categorize Satanism in the modern era as essentially an *anti-morality movement*, or a *do-whatever-you-want-to-do* type of society within society.

From that point, the Passantinos opened the door to what they believed to be the apparent *misconceptions* regarding Satanism. They made statements like, "*Most contemporary witchcraft groups are matriarchal and emphasize the feminine aspect of reality.*" They then take pains to disprove those beliefs. They do so with other statements such as, "*There is no substantiation for this view, and it is contradicted by the historical evidence.*"[1]

They take the statement that "*Witchcraft is condemned in the Bible*" to ultimately mean that what God *really meant* was that "*Biblical refer-*

---

[1] Bob and Gretchen Passantino *Satanism* (Zondervan, 1995), 45

ences refer more to practices than to beliefs or worship."[2] This avoids the sin of the "heart" though, and Scripture does not do that. It appears then that the Passantinos have changed the *meaning* of Scripture to suit their own presuppositions.

In the end, their book on Satanism says little to nothing about Satanism. While it is recognized that many Satanists do *not* believe in an actual being called Satan, some certainly do.

Had I written a book such as the one the Passantinos wrote on Satanism, my concern would be not only *how* others reviewed it, but also by *whom* it was reviewed as well. Diana Vera has a website on the subject of "Theistic Satanism" and there she explores many of the beliefs and meanings of various Satanists and groups.

It is interesting to note that Vera speaks highly of the Passantino's book. On her site, under the heading, "*Some rare Christians who helped end the SRA scare*," she lists the following:

- *In 1992, the evangelical Christian magazine Cornerstone published a series of articles exposing several sensationalistic tales about Satanism as frauds. One was Mike Warnke's tale, exposed by Cornerstone writers **Jon Trott** and Mike Hertenstein.* **Trott and Hertenstein later expanded their article into a book, Selling Satan**.
- *Also in the early 1990's, a Christian apologetics ministry known as the Christian Research Institute published some articles skeptical toward the SRA scare, including The Hard Facts About Satanic Ritual Abuse by* **Bob and Gretchen Passantino** *in 1992.*
- *Back in 1986, when the SRA scare was still a rising trend, the Christian Research Institute had published "The Many Faces of Satanism? by Craig S. Hawkins. That article didn't do anything*

---

[2] Ibid

> to debunk the SRA scare, but it was nevertheless a relatively sane article, as evangelical Christian writings on Satanism go, given when it was written.
> - **Bob and Gretchen Passantino wrote some SRA-debunking articles for Cornerstone too** and on their own "Answers in Action" website, as well as for the Christian Research Institute. (See my comments on various writings by the Passantinos.)"[3]

Frankly, I would be concerned if someone who thought of himself or herself as a Theistic Satanist reviewed my work *favorably*. However, Vera does not stop there. Though she *does* state that she has some serious concerns about the comments they have made in print, she continues with some glowing comments about the Passantinos on a special page on her Web site.

"Gretchen Passantino and her late husband Bob are among the very few evangelical Christian writers who really do seem to care about truthfulness regarding other religions. In the early 1990's, they took what was then a very courageous stand against the "Satanic Ritual Abuse" scare. They and their webmaster John Baskette wrote articles exposing some of the earliest alleged cases of SRA (Lauren Stratford and Rebecca Brown) as fraudulent. Some articles of theirs were published in the evangelical Christian magazine Cornerstone, whose staff writers Jon Trott and Mike Hertenstein debunked Mike Warnke's 'ex-Satanist' claims in 1992.

*"**I very much do appreciate their work in opposing the SRA scare**. Most of the articles on their Satanism and SRA page are well-researched critiques of various SRA scaremongers. There's also a very informative article Satanic Ritual Abuse in Popular Christian Literature, Why Christians Fall for a Lie Searching for the Truth, containing a*

---

[3] http://theisticsatanism.com/popular/witchhunt/XianPanic.html

brief history of the SRA scare in Christian literature."[4] (emphasis added)

Regarding the problems she has with some of what the Passantinos have published and pass off as fact, Vera states, *"However, their article When the Devil Dares: Teenagers and Satanism contains quite a few questionable claims of its own."*[5]

She continues by stating, *"'When the Devil Dares' contains **lots of generalizations** about teenage Satanists. (Examples: 'Most teenagers who practice Satanism also abuse drugs and alcohol and are sexually promiscuous,' and 'Satanism is an indicator of serious personal dysfunction.') **I wonder where all these generalizations came from**, and what they were based on."*[6] (emphasis added)

Vera goes onto say, *"I'll give the Passantinos the benefit of the doubt and assume that they used the best information that was easily available to them at that time. It would be very difficult for anyone to do a truly scientific survey of teenage Satanists, given that most Satanists -- especially most teenage Satanists -- have existed only as isolated individuals and small groups. The few public 'Satanic churches' were not representative of all Satanists, and it does not appear that the Passantinos' article was based on them anyway. Only now, thanks to the Internet, is a larger community of Satanists in general -- including theistic Satanists -- finally starting to emerge. Perhaps a truly scientific survey of Satanists may finally become possible, for the first time ever, in a few years from now."*[7]

Vera is right to wonder about *where* the Passantinos got their information. One cannot help speculate about the Passantinos and their claim of integrity and investigative journalism. It almost appears as

---

[4] http://theisticsatanism.com/popular/witchhunt/Passantino.html
[5] Ibid
[6] Ibid
[7] Ibid

though they made it up as they went, doing their level best to *downplay* any real concerns about Satanism as a religion and a societal problem. This makes their connection with Cornerstone Magazine even more questionable, regarding the articles that were published through the magazine.

Cornerstone Magazine
Cornerstone magazine originated as a newsletter and later a magazine, published by Jesus People, USA (JPUSA). It grew out of the Jesus People Movement, which was a type of Christianized hippie movement. Many of the articles were about the drug culture, conversions and other related stories. Eventually, in the late 80s, JPUSA joined with the Evangelical Covenant Church.

Apparently, the JPUSA has had its own critics, shining the light on some of the alleged abuses within the church itself. Interestingly enough, an article appeared on the 'Net, which criticized the way the writers of Cornerstone magazine had reviewed a book by Dr. Ronald Enroth (*Recovering for Churches that Abuse*, a follow up to his first book, *Churches That Abuse*). Though the elders of the Jesus People congregation attempted to persuade Enroth to edit his book, leaving out or playing down any mention of abuses within JPUSA, he refused and the first book went to print.

JPUSA members condemned the book, believing it to be filled with untruths, or at least exaggerations. During this same period of time, the Charismatic Movement had really picked up steam, gaining quite a burgeoning membership, if you will. This author was one of those people who became involved in that movement, reading books by many of authors affiliated with it, including Jamie Buckingham. It turns out Jamie Buckingham was *also* a member of the JPUSA.

Investigative Journalism?
What is more than interesting though, is that the writers and staff at Cornerstone magazine, (and remember, Cornerstone *came out* of the

JPUSA), who were supposed to be *investigative* journalists and had brought down people like Warnke, Stratton, and Brown, were now under the microscope. Though they attempted to give the impression that this did not bother them, it was clear that they did not appreciate or welcome that type of scrutiny.

When they heard about Enroth's *second* book, they decided to review it. In fact, they set aside 15½ pages in one of their issues for that purpose. What is wrong with that? Nothing *if* the book had actually been published at that point. Instead, they reviewed a book that had *not* been published yet, based solely on the correspondence they had between themselves and Dr. Enroth!

As a preamble to their review, Cornerstone magazine published an editorial about that issue with the review of Enroth's book. They said in part, *"This issue of Cornerstone has been an especially hard one for us to put together--not only because of thirty-two extra pages, but mainly because we will be bringing to our readers charges made against us by Dr. Ronald Enroth.* **We have been led to believe through correspondence with Dr. Enroth, a respected author and former colleague in cult-watching, that he intends to voice allegations against Jesus People USA Covenant Church (JPUSA)***, Cornerstone's parent ministry, in a forthcoming* Zondervan book, Recovering from Churches That Abuse. **The title says it all, doesn't it?** *Or perhaps it doesn't. Zondervan advertised this book, which we are likely to be included in, this way: 'The seriousness of the problem of abusive sects was driven home by the tragedy this past spring at the Branch Davidian compound. In his new book, Recovering from Churches That Abuse, Enroth responds to the problems created by such groups and points the way towards spiritual and emotional healing for those who have come out of them.' To say we were shocked by this would be an understatement."*[8] (emphasis added)

---

[8] http://www.cornerstonemag.com/features/iss103/acidtest.htm

As if this was not enough, the editorial went onto say, "**Those who have followed this magazine will recognize that we have increasingly focused on investigative reporting, constantly seeking to maintain biblical standards of integrity and accountability.** Therefore, when the spotlight is turned on us, **it is only fitting that we should disclose our own inner workings in the same manner of relentless honesty**--or, as our advertising department likes to say, with the same commitment to 'raw truth.' In keeping with the high premium we place on being accountable to the body of Christ at large and to our denomination, the Evangelical Covenant Church, we present the problem--as best we understand it--to you, our friends and readers."[9] (emphasis added)

Breaking the Law?

The editorial continues at length commenting on the many facets of communication between the staff at Cornerstone and Dr. Enroth. In fact, many quotes are pulled directly from some of the correspondence that passed between the two parties. Since it was done without Enroth's permission, what they did actually amounts to a crime, as Dr. Enroth notes. *"Attorneys familiar with intellectual property law have clearly indicated that personal correspondence is covered by copyright, according to Section 102(a), Section 107, and Section 202 of the Copyright Act of 1976. There is legal precedent set forth in a number of cases, including Salinger v. Random House. The extensive use of my personal correspondence, without my knowledge or consent, amounts to "trial by correspondence." More seriously, it appears to be a violation of the law. I hold author Jon Trott, editors Anson Shupe, William A. Stacey, and Susan E. Darnell, together with New York University Press, jointly responsible for what appears to be careless disregard for copyright law. Readers of this response should also know that the leadership of the Evangelical Covenant Church, heretofore fully supportive of JPUSA, were not apprised of Trott's use of their correspondence or*

---

[9] http://www.cornerstonemag.com/features/iss103/acidtest.htm

mine. *In a letter to me dated September 1, 2000, Dr. Glenn R. Palmberg, the current president of the ECC, stated that the leadership of that denomination neither authorized nor consented to the distribution of the correspondence, which Trott so frequently mentions in his essay."*[10]

A good question to ask at this point is if the folks at Cornerstone magazine considered themselves to be *accountable* and essentially *above board*, how could they make such an imprudent slip by breaking the law? Dr. Enroth accuses Jon Trott and other Cornerstone staff writers of being *adversarial* and employing *illegal* tactics. It appears that he may have a case. While the average person might not be aware that quoting from letters without permission is a crime, certainly those who consider themselves to be investigative journalists should have known better.

Dr. Roth's book alleges that within the JPUSA, there were problems of *abuse*, involving *authoritarian rule, legalism, manipulation, intimidation,* and other things as well. When his books came out, a number of people had left the JPUSA. As time progressed, a greater exodus was taking place from those involved in the JPUSA. Individuals from Wellspring Retreat and Resource Center have confirmed all of this. In fact, in reference to JPUSA, they stated, *"In recent years, however, we have been in contact with several people who have left the group recently. These were long-time members of JPUSA, some as long as 20 years, who gave us credible reports of spiritual abuse they suffered from the leadership while in JPUSA. These alleged incidents were not just in the distant past, but right up to the present. These reports greatly disturb us, and we stand ready to assist these and other former members in any way we can."*[11]

Rick Ross has spent years gathering information on JPUSA, and apparently spent ten years of his life *with* them. He states, *"As a mem-*

---

[10] http://www.rickross.com/reference/jesuspeople/jp2.html
[11] http://www.rickross.com/reference/jesuspeople/jesuspeople4.

ber of JPUSA it is difficult to realize that it is not proper or normal for someone in leadership to tell you:

- *You and your spouse must first ask permission to have children.*
- *You don't see anything wrong with an elder telling you how you can have sexual relations with your wife and the frequency of those relations.*
- *You believe the justifications on why someone in leadership will decide on whom you can associate with, visit or marry.*
- *As a member you learn not to question the different lifestyles, bank accounts, or property that elders have--compared to regular members.*
- *You unlearn that no one has the right to force you into an unwanted or dangerous occupation or deprive you of an education--especially when you are paying for theirs.*
- *You become comfortable with the rule that an approved fellow member must always accompany you when leaving the premises.*
- *You accept as fact without question that your self-appointed leaders are 'more godly' than you and can be trusted when you confess your sins, desires, secrets, and problems to them.*
- *You rationalize with them when they tell others these things and use them against you.*
- *You learn to do the same to others for the good of 'The community'.*"[12]

Not sure what the reader thinks about that, but from this author's perspective, those are some of the very things that create cults and it all begins with *control*. If you control a person's beliefs, you control *them*. In fact, it appears as though JPUSA is a miniature version of

---

[12] http://www.rickross.com/reference/jesuspeople/JPUSA_letter3.html

what the world's elite wants to do to the citizens of the entire world. It seems at least to Ross, that JPUSA is big on *control*. Is it any wonder that Dr. Enroth wrote books in which he questioned the practices of JPUSA, among other groups?

The reality of this entire saga seems to sum itself up quite nicely like this:

- *The JPUSA is a group that controls its adherents*

- *They have strange views on what it means to be a Christian and the role of leaders within Christianity over the "flock"*

- *JPUSA gave rise to Cornerstone Magazine*

- *Cornerstone Magazine spent time castigating those with whom they did not agree, such as Mike Warnke, Lauren Stratford, and Rebecca Brown*

- *During the same time as the JPUSA, the Charismatic Movement was making huge inroads into American churches*

- *It is common knowledge to anyone who is not afraid of the truth that many excesses and much error occurred and often ran rampant within the Charismatic Movement*

- *If error did/does exist within the movement, the error could have only one source – Satan*

- *If Satan was the source of the error as well as the controlling factor within the JPUSA, it stands to reason that many of these individuals were standing on sandy ground*

- *If they were standing on sandy ground, they had no foundation at all, having themselves been deceived by error*

- *If they were deceived by error, that means that Satan and his minions had at least partial hold on many of these individuals*

- *If Satan had hold on them, it is obvious then that he called the shots and had every reason to work through people to downplay the Satanic scare that existed in those years*

- *Having squelched by discrediting people, the entire area of Satanism became something no credible person wanted to touch for the sake of their own reputation and their family.*

The Fox and the Chicken

It appears that staff or freelance writers associated with Cornerstone magazine, spent time and effort in debunking the testimony of other Christians. The problem of course is that it appears as though the fox was guarding the chicken coop because while they were busy ferreting out *other* people with what they felt were problems of credibility their own problems remained unchecked. Such is often the case with individuals who are unable to see the board in their own eye, but can and do easily notice and point out the speck in someone else's eye. In spite of their words pledging that they deemed it not only important, but also highly valuable to be under the microscope, they actually did not like it when someone took them up on it and placed them under scrutiny.

So what is the point? Why have I bothered to share this information in my opening chapter? Because it is extremely important that you – the reader – understand that this book is about subjects that you will not find pleasant and you need to know what is at stake. While not pleasant, they are presented carefully and conscientiously, in such a way as to keep sensationalism to a minimum. Even so, some of what appears here will seem sensational. That cannot be helped because of the nature of the events themselves.

When Cornerstone magazine decided to take the time to go after people like Warnke, Stratton, and Brown, they did so with *relish* and they may have done so based on a push from another "source." In those days, it was as if anyone who said anything about the existence of Satanism (negatively) was immediately *questioned*, *doubted*, and then roundly *castigated*.

In essence, it became the witch-hunt of the day. Professing Christians were going after other Christians, all in the name of *truth*. Whose truth? Cornerstone's? Jon Trott's? The Passantinos? Referring back to that period it is obvious that a great deal of *error* existed within the visible Church. This error gave rise to more of the same and all done in the name of God.

Meanwhile, people who actually came out of a background steeped in Satanism and satanic ritual were called liars and thieves. They were liars because their books were allegedly filled with created scenarios that did not happen, and thieves because they were allegedly making themselves rich from lies. Never mind that numerous law enforcement officials found much truth in their books because they had seen with their own eyes the results of many of these ritual killings.

That was the 1970s and 80s and even somewhat into the 90s, when the reality of Satanism was downplayed. However, does it not make sense that *if* Satan has been creating a network of worshipers who involve themselves in rituals that require the torture/killing of animals *and* even human beings, that he would also do everything possible to cover it up *if* that information ever started coming to light?

It does not take a rocket scientist to review history to see that people who have been involved in worshiping Satan (through various gods like Molech, or Baal, or others), have often sacrificed either animals or humans to that god. It is clear from the Old Testament alone that this was often the case. Molech (Satan by another name) accepted the offering of children (babies to young adults) as *appeasement*. Every known culture has records of ritualistic sacrifices and killings, both of animals and human beings.

Do people really believe that because humanity is supposedly civilized, men and women are somehow above becoming involved in something so lurid and uncivilized? If Jeffrey Dahmer were still alive, we could ask him why he tortured, killed, and *cannibalized* numerous *human* victims. We could ask him why he loved watching *The Exorcist*, and how his personality changed while watching it (this according to one survivor). There have been many other perpetrators as well. Since the 1970s and 80s, there have been too many victims, too many perpetrators, and too many missing children and adults that have never been found to continue downplaying the role of Satan in any of this. Only the naïve continue to disbelieve in the covert activities of Satanists.

Some of the arguments the Cornerstone writers used against Lauren Stratton was that her memory was not consistent. Biting my tongue to keep from being sarcastic, *if* Stratton was a victim of the many things she states, is it possible that her memory *might* have been just a bit *fractured*? It is *very* possible.

The Charismatic Movement, Jamie Buckingham and Others
A concern arises regarding the credibility of some of the other writers in the 1980s and 90s, mainly because of the emphasis on the *sign gifts* of the Holy Spirit. There were many authors during that time who claimed to witness many miracles of one sort or another, yet no proof was provided as to their efficacy. Readers were left to simply take the word of the individual authors or not since nothing was ever substantiated.

When this author was involved in the Charismatic Movement years ago, many books became some of the Christian best sellers of the time. Books by Jamie Buckingham, Merlin Carouthers, Charles and Frances Hunter (The Happy Hunters), Frank Foglio, Bob Mumford, Harold Hill (Kings Kids), and others became household names. Their books often spoke of God's power in healing, guiding, and the everyday miracle that Christians during that time were taught to expect.

I still recall some of the testimonies presented as fact by these authors. In one book, one author speaks of being in the hospital with a dear friend who was near death. In the room with him were a few friends, nurses, and a doctor. After some time, the man on his deathbed *did* indeed pass from this life to the next.

The author stated that he immediately claimed by faith the ability to raise that dead man to life. He *commanded* in the Name of Jesus that the man should return to his body and live again. If Jesus did it with Lazarus, then followers of Jesus also have that power too, we were to believe.

According to the author, the man *did* start to revive, to the absolute surprise of the medical staff and the others in the room. As everyone waited, the man opened his eyes, looked at the author, and gently shook his head from side to side, signifying that he did not want to come back. At that point, he left his body and passed to the next life.

Did that actually happen? The author said it did, so it must have happened, right? It could not be that the author *thought* it happened, or that the man had not completely died and when the author began yelling at the top of his lungs that the man should rise from the dead, he actually heard him, opened his eyes, and signaled, "no."

Did The Events Really Happen?
How do we know without doubt that it took place? As far as this author can recall, there was no avadavat, signed by the medical staff and included in that book. There was no other testimony from friends who were there either. What we have is the *stated* word of one individual and that is all.

Jamie Buckingham in his book *Miracle Power*, relates an incident in his preface in which while working on something at home, the screwdriver he was using slipped and resulted in a severe gouge in his hand. Instinctively, he pulled the screwdriver out and wound up tearing away more flesh, he related. Not only was he pain but also bleeding from the "*deep, open wound.*"[13]

He relates that he went to the floor and after asking himself what Jesus would do if He were present, he realized that Jesus would likely *heal* him. Since Jesus was not there physically, but *was* living inside Buckingham, then why wouldn't Jesus heal *through* Buckingham? He began praying. "*Gradually, as I prayed, I lost track of time. The pain subsided and I was vaguely aware the bleeding had stopped. But my wound was no longer the major issue. I was lost in the wonder of the prayer, no longer praying for healing, simply 'communing' with God. The Heavenly Father was there and the Holy Spirit in me was having fellowship with Him.*"[14]

Buckingham continues by explaining that after a few minutes, he removed his hand from over the wounded hand to see what was there. Here is what he saw, in his own words. "*The spot between my thumb and forefinger where the ragged screwdriver had penetrated was still covered with blood...As I wiped away the blood I was aware the wound had closed. Not only had it closed, it had healed over. There was no gaping hole, no cut, not even an indentation.* **All I could see was a tiny scar, like a wrinkle in my hand**. *My wife examined my hand, also. It was healed.*"[15] (emphasis added)

All right, let's look at what Buckingham stated. He said he was "healed," yet he also says that there was virtually nothing left from the wound except a "tiny scar." Hmmm, now I am trying to recall any place in the Bible where God healed someone and left a *scar*. Maybe I have missed it somewhere in Holy Writ, but for the life of me, I cannot recall a place where God healed someone and a telltale sign of the previous problem *remained*. But maybe I'm just being way too picky.

---

[13] Jamie Buckingham *Miracle Power* (Vine Books 1988), ix
[14] Ibid, x
[15] Ibid, x

In another section of Buckingham's book, he talks about physical healings. He states, *"First of all – you have the power to bestow the word of God on somebody else. That power and authority is resident within you. You don't have to call for the experts. Second – you have the right to receive the word of God when it comes into your life – and be healed. Circumstances may or may not change, but healing comes through God's word, not through circumstances. We are to accept it even when circumstances seem to deny it. Miracles always defy logic and human understanding. Miracles occur to show men that the Kingdom of God is here. Present. It is a silent Kingdom operating in this universe. Without miracles, there is no proof that God is any bigger than we are. We need miracles to show men that there is a God "out there" who not only created us, but who cares for us – and is still in control of all the natural laws."*[16]

Aside from the fact that Buckingham has stated that Christians have a right to be healed, don't need to go to doctors, miracles happen to prove that God exists, and prove that the Kingdom of God is present, there is nothing wrong theologically with anything he stated!

Those Happy Hunters
Charles and Frances Hunter, in their book *Miracles, Miracles, Miracles*, they speak of one miracle after the other that apparently took place in their lives. Can we believe them? *Should* we believe them?

In fact, the Hunters have a number of books out, one entitled *How to Heal the Sick*, which is a book that...explains in easy steps how to heal the sick! The book begins with this statement, *"We have been assigned and commissioned to take the gospel to all the world around us, and the only way we will be able to accomplish this is with miracles just like Jesus did!"*[17]

---

[16] Jamie Buckingham *Miracle Power* (Vine Books 1988), 114
[17] Charles and Frances Hunter *How to Heal the Sick* (Whitaker House 2000), 17

Their theology is interesting, but nowhere in the Great Commission do I read where God said we would be doing miracles just like Jesus did, or that in order to fulfill the Great Commission, it would *require* miracles. The greatest miracle that God has ever done and continues to do is to *save a soul*! That is the miracle that *transforms* a life.

They continue in their book stating, "*This book will teach YOU how to heal the sick in the name of Jesus, and to give GOD all the glory! You will also learn that if one method doesn't work for you, you should try another way, because if God had wanted US to heal only one particular way, he would never have had Jesus heal in so many different ways in the Bible!*"[18] Actually, the healings that Jesus performed attested to *His deity*. He did not do those miracles as a way of teaching His followers how to do them. Of course, the other point to be made here is that WE do not heal anyone! IF there is a healing, it is because God did it, period.

In a book titled *Holy Laughter*, the Hunters explain the phenomenon that (at that time) was sweeping through many worship services across the globe. This *Holy Laughter*, they said, was God "*restoring the joy of our salvation to the end-time church!*"[19] At one point in their book after quoting Acts 2:11-19 (which is where Peter refers to the prophet Joel, noting in part that God will show wonders in heaven and on the earth), the Hunters state, "*And one of today's signs 'in the earth beneath' is the 'holy laughter' which is supernaturally overcoming people in services all over the world!*"[20] Frankly, it is difficult to determine how they make that connection, because there is nothing in Scripture that agrees with their opinion on this. There is nothing in Scripture that describes people falling down and laughing themselves silly as some type of evidence of God's presence. In fact, it appears that Scripture teaches an abject fear of God even for the saved!

---

[18] Charles and Frances Hunter *How to Heal the Sick* (Whitaker House 2000), 19
[19] Ibid, back cover
[20] Charles and Frances Hunter *Holy Laughter* (Hunter Books 1994), 7

Frank "Hey God" Foglio

In Frank Foglio's book *Hey God!*, he writes of the numerous miracles that God performed after he, his mother, and other family members became Christians and were then reportedly, *baptized* with the Holy Spirit. This included lots of wind and tongues.

On one occasion, there was a large group of people gathered at Frank's home. His mother was in the kitchen cooking and realized that she had hardly any spaghetti noodles left, not nearly enough to feed the entire crowd of people. What could she do? She ran to her Bible, opened it up to one of the passages where Jesus fed thousands of people, and looking up to heaven said, "*Hey God! You make spaghetti!*" It was her way (in her broken English) of asking God to perform that same type of miracle. (Somehow, going from a deeply respectful Catholic to being baptized with the Spirit meant not having to show God anymore respect.)

In an alleged act of faith, the mother got the biggest pot she could find, filled it with water, and then put in the noodles that she *did* have. They disappeared from view as soon as they hit the water.

According to Frank, as time went on, the mother busied herself with other preparations coming back to stir the water occasionally. Eventually it was time to feed everyone, and so the mother served the spaghetti. To Frank's own astonishment, Frank's mother was able to serve more noodles than he thought she should have been able to do so. It seemed as though they would never end and as it turned out, there was plenty of spaghetti for everyone, with a great deal of it left over. Frank was understandably amazed at what he had just seen.

Did this event really happen? There is no way to know because unless you were there, no one knows. We are left to either believe Foglio's testimony or not. His book has numerous events and situations in which God seemingly performed specific miracles just for them and in ways in which they would understand what God was telling them.

There was another time when God allegedly slapped Foglio's father in the face with His big, "white hand" that came down from the sky. Foglio senior had quit smoking cigars prior, yet the enemy had begun tempting him to smoke again. After rolling a cigar around in his mouth, the temptation came to "light up the cigar" and that is when the hand came out of the sky. Apparently, there was enough force to knock Foglio senior into the wall of the barn and cut his lip. He ran into the house explaining that God had hit him.

Did it happen? Who knows, but logic indicates it did *not*. Since there is no way to verify it, it remains as is, with a question mark over it.

This is a big problem with people believing in miracles and sign gifts for today. It turns out to be *their* word against anyone else's. This is not to say that God does not perform miracles today, but of course, the greatest miracle that He performs on a daily basis is bringing a new person into His Kingdom. All other miracles pale in comparison, yet it seems that the sign miracles seemed to have greater emphasis within the Charismatic Movement, not salvation. Certainly, that was important, but what was *more* important was seeing how God worked every day in the lives of His children. That was seen in the form of miracle after miracle, as if God only wants to "wow" us with the splendor of His power. I can gain that from seeing Creation.

Truth with Error
It is a well-known fact that the Charismatic Movement tends to open itself up to, and embrace, *error*. The reason for this is due to the emphasis on sign gifts and prophetic mutterings. During this author's time involved in the movement, seeming miracles occurred, people spoke in tongues, healings took place, and many prophetic utterances were given, the latter usually called a *word of knowledge*.

In recalling those events, it seems clear that many of the words of knowledge given were essentially reiterated Scripture. Many of the "words" from Scripture were certainly wonderful since they were from God's Word. The problem though is that people often seemed to place great emphasis on those particular words (out of context), as if the remainder of the Bible was not as important.

Moreover, somehow most of these words became the catalyst for believing that God was pouring out His Spirit on humanity afresh and that we should expect great, powerful, and wonderful things that God was going to do. Each meeting or worship service became a time of intense and exciting *expectancy*.

Unlike the claims of Satanism by some, the difficulty remains though that rarely if ever were claims of miracles viewed with a *critical* eye. The reason for that was that it was believed that everything that *sounded* or *looked* "good" must have been from God. Nothing evil could have been from God. Many of these miraculous testimonies from people were simply accepted without question.

This is not the way that the Bible tells us to discern the spirits. We are to test them (1 John 4:1), to determine their truthfulness. If we simply accept what they say as truth without question, we are opening ourselves up to error and error has often (and unfortunately), been a keynote of the Charismatic Movement.

Please understand, if you are involved in the Charismatic Movement, certainly that is your right. However, in all honestly, you must admit that there are excesses in that movement, which have caused people to go way beyond the Lord's will, and into places of error.

Every few years there seems to have been something *new* from within the Charismatic Movement. It was not long before the world came to know that "holy laughter" was apparently a joyous overflowing from God that literally bubbled over into laughter. There are videos on the Internet in which people spend their entire time laughing during *worship* services. They roll on the floor, fall over onto the person next to them, or belly laugh themselves silly.

God's Bartender?
Dr. Rodney Howard Browne has long been known as "God's Bartender" because wherever he goes, "holy laughter" or some other type of alleged spiritual empowering said to be from God follows. Videos that highlight some of these things show people simply laughing. There is no preaching, there is no teaching, nor is the Bible hardly referenced. Yet, God allegedly pours out blessing on people and they *laugh, laugh, and laugh some more.*

What is gained from that? Besides *feelings*, what is truly gained? How is God glorified? Why can't these things be from the enemy of our souls? Answer: they easily *could* be, but are rarely credited to Satan. In fact, those who have the temerity to question the source are roundly criticized and often ostracized. Though the Bible tells us to question and seek discernment, those within the Charismatic Movement tell us we should *not*.

To have a worship service where all people do is sit around laughing their heads off is *nothing* but anti-God expression! There is nothing in that environment that engenders a deeper love, respect, or reverence for God. It simply makes people *feel* good about *themselves*.

Where are the John Trotts, the Passantinos and others from Cornerstone Magazine to comment on this trend? Why were they and many others seemingly unconcerned about these excesses? Did they take the time to shine the light of journalistic integrity, credibility, and discernment onto these events, or on author Jamie Buckingham's books, or Frank Foglio's, or other authors? As noted, since Jamie Buckingham was part of the Jesus People Movement, he would likely have received no such concern.

Why should we simply take the word of someone who claims that God's big, white hand slapped his father across the face? Why should we simply take it for granted that it must be true when Harold Hill claims that a NASA space engineer figured out mathematically that when Elijah prayed that the earth would stand still for a day, it *did* and can be proven? This has actually been debunked.

Why should we believe what the Hunters tell us about how often they experienced God's miracles on a near-daily basis? Where's the proof? Why are we expected to accept it with no questions asked, yet when it comes to Satanism, we must bring out the big guns to get to the bottom of it? This makes no sense.

Would Satan *Stoop* to Work Both Ends Against the Middle?
Could there be a possibility – however remote – that Satan is merely working both sides against the middle? Why could he not be the source of Satanism with its ritualistic torture and killings, while at the same time be the source of *much* within the Charismatic Movement? Of course, those within the Charismatic Movement would not like that suggestion, but point out from Scripture why Satan could not be the author of *both*.

We know that there have been many cases of strange tongues among third world tribes. We also know that witch doctors can and have cast demons out of people and allegedly healed people. This is not odd at all. In fact, in Scripture, we see this very thing at work in the Old as well as New Testaments (Witch of Endor, Seven Sons of Sceva, and Moses and the wise men of Pharaoh's court).

Satan, who is a very powerful being, has the ability to imitate a good deal that may appear as though it came from God, when in point of fact, simply came from Satan. Jesus Himself said that Satan's house will not stand because it is *divided* (cf. Matthew 12:25). It is obvious that Satan *is* playing both ends against the middle in order to deceive.

Could it be that Jon Trott and the Passantinos either knowingly or unknowingly were deceived into thinking that the Satanism that was rising to the surface through people like Warnke, Stratford and others, was faked? If so, they then felt it their obligation to stamp it out. However, when it came to what was happening within the Charismatic Movement, they felt no such need when it came to any of the *excesses* that led to error there? It is *more* than possible.

Trott has an interesting background to say the least and it becomes clear that he often has an axe to grind and his demeanor is often overtly nasty. Apologetics Index has this to say, "*Jon Trott, the magazine's current senior editor, uncritically accepts the views of cult apologists - and actively promotes their work. Like the cult defenders whose work he admires, he attacks those who use proper terminology such as 'cult' and cult apologist. He also objects to the identification of the Church of Scientology as a 'hate group,' even though hate and harassment activities are specifically condoned and encouraged in that organization's scripture (and consequently evidenced in the group's behavior).*"[21]

Trott prefers not to label the Church of Scientology as a hate group in spite of their known tactics around the world. Further, Apologetics Index says, "*Though Trott apparently has little practical experience in dealing with actual current and former cult members, and is not considered to be a cult expert, he vehemently defends his views, often getting downright nasty in the process.*"

Faith Healers as a *Profession*?
Another thing to realize is that not only was the Charismatic Movement a force to be reckoned with, but also faith healers like Kathryn Kuhlman, Oral Roberts and others were well known and had celebrity status. What they taught, said, and did was not questioned by those who followed them. For the most part, they were viewed as

---

[21] http://www.apologeticsindex.org/c135.html

people who had a special relationship with God that gave them the ability to heal. People from all over the world came to their services in the hopes of receiving healing.

However, it should be noted that Kuhlman's as well as Roberts' theology is often questionable to say the least, even bordering on the *mystical*. Both of these individuals were also not without credibility problems, which seemed to dog them for years. Yet few if any within the Charismatic Movement questioned their integrity or veracity.

In the case of Kuhlman, she was sued by her personal administrator, *"who claimed she kept $1 million in jewelry and $1 million in fine art hidden away and sued her for $430,500 for breach of contract. Two former associates accused her in the lawsuit of diverting funds and illegally removing records, which she denied and said the records were not private. According to Kuhlman, the lawsuit was settled prior to trial."*[22]

Though Kuhlman is credited with an untold number of healings, there has been no substantiated evidence that even one person was in fact permanently healed through her ministry. *"Many accounts of healings were published in her books, which were 'ghost-written' by author **Jamie Buckingham** of Florida, including her autobiography, which was dictated at a hotel in Las Vegas. Buckingham also wrote his own Kuhlman biography that presented an unvarnished account of her life."*[23] (emphasis added)

Of course, Oral Roberts came to be known as the faith healer whom God had apparently "blackmailed" by telling him (in the form of a 900 foot vision of Jesus), that he must raise eight million dollars, or God was going to *"call him home."* He wound up raising just over nine million dollars because of it.

---

[22] http://en.wikipedia.org/wiki/Kathryn_Kuhlman
[23] Ibid

There are of course a few problems with that whole story. First, why would *any* authentic believer be *afraid* to go home to heaven? Secondly, why would God deliberately *blackmail* any of His children? Third, why did people give simply because Oral Roberts presented a story to them that was very likely based on a lie? There is only one answer.

Satanism is Out There
The book that you are now reading goes under the assumption that Satanism, Satanic crime, and Satanic Ritual Abuse (SRA) are *real*. This author believes that much of what is said to have happened in the 1970s (and before) *did* happen, and it has continued since then. What you will read in this book is true, as far as this author can discern. However, whether anyone believes the situations herein described or not, the question needs to be asked: *is Satan capable of spearheading a campaign in which people are ritualistically killed during the process of worship*?

We have seen evidence of it in history and in recent years, with groups like *Santeria*, as well as others devoted to Satan. This evidence countermands what Cornerstone Magazine, and others had to say about Satanism then. We will take some time to look closely at what many of these groups stand for, what they attempt to accomplish, and how they go through the process of bringing their wishes to fulfillment in their desire to serve their master, Satan.

We also need to be aware of the fact that Satanism though often strictly and narrowly defined, often has a far *wider scope*. In this book, Satanism is understood to mean *anything* that Satan creates in which he attempts to *compel* people to follow *him* and move *away* from *God*. In another book – *Demons in Disguise* – we included a chart called "Satan's Wheel of UN-fortune." Because of its importance to this topic, we have also included it in this book on page 34.

There are many paths that Satan has created that trick people into following him. We *must* understand that whether people know they are following Satan or not, they are *still* following him. If they are following him, they are *worshiping* him. This is what Satan has promised to do since he fell. He declared that he would make his throne higher than God's (cf. Isaiah 14:12-15). This is the goal that started him off on the wrong path altogether.

If we consider the fact that Satan meant a number of things when those thoughts were found within him, we will come to grasp the full scope of Satanism. It is not merely relegated to overt worship of Satan. When Satan fell because he actually intended to raise himself up above God, he saw that happening by:

- *Getting all the world to worship him (Satan) instead of God*
- *Tricking people by providing what they want so that they will be worshiping him by default*
- *Keeping them from going to God for salvation*

Satan Has Always Been Working Toward His Goals
Satan set out his goals clearly way back before this earth was ever made. He said he would raise his throne above God's throne. The temerity of a *created* being believing that he could become *better* than the One who created him is outrageous!

Besides the angelic hosts who followed him in rebellion, Satan set his eyes on this world and human beings, which were the pinnacle of God's creative efforts. Though we say "efforts," there was no effort on God's part at all. It took no energy, no effort, but we describe it in human terms to better understand it.

Since Satan saw that God had created the earth, the animals, separated the seas from the mountains and finally created man, Satan

Satan's Wheel of UN-Fortune

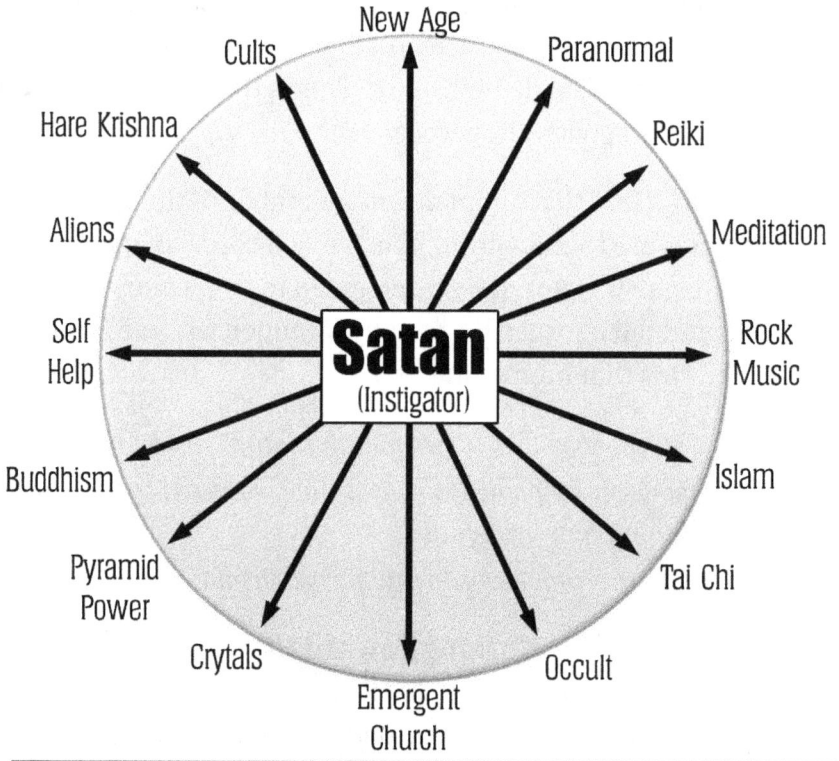

New Age, Cults, Paranormal, Hare Krishna, Reiki, Aliens, Meditation, Self Help, **Satan (Instigator)**, Rock Music, Buddhism, Islam, Pyramid Power, Tai Chi, Crytals, Occult, Emergent Church

Satan has created something for everyone, in order to <u>seduce</u> and <u>enslave</u>. The above is only a sampling. What may not work for one, will work for another. All ways lead the world to the same ultimate climax, which is a one-world government, led by a one-world ruler. Satan will finally get his chance to rule over God's Creation, but not for long.

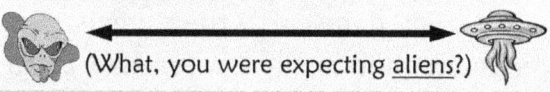

Welcome to <u>Your</u> Afterlife!

You're gonna HATE it here! Oh well...

(What, you were expecting <u>aliens</u>?)

©2010 F. DERUVO

knew that in order to bring his goals to fruition, he would be required to gain man's *loyalty*. Satan would have to wrest man's love and loyalty for God away from God, turning it to him (Satan). If he could get our first parents to do this, the act of disobedience would penetrate the entire race of human beings. In doing so then, when all is said and done, he would hope to have a greater body of beings who worshiped him (Satan) than God had who worshiped Him.

Satan's plan has been and remains made up of a multitude of paths that pull people away from God. Satan does not care if they worship him with sacrifices, or worship him by attempting to become the biggest drug supplier in the world. He does not care if they worship him by trafficking in human beings, or if they create a vast empire of pornography.

Satan could care less *how* people worship him. What he cares about is that they do not worship *God* and remain free of salvation. If Satan can keep people from worshiping God, then they are worshiping him (Satan) by default. That is how it works and that is how it *has* worked since Satan fell from grace. There is nothing mysterious about this, yet people have been convinced that Satanism by its nature must only be *torture* leading up to *ritualistic killings* of animals or human beings. This is not true. That is only *one form* of Satanism and while this book explores that area, other avenues are explored that have not often been thought of as Satanism.

It is <u>All</u> Satanism in One Form or Another
For instance, the drug culture has simply been the "drug culture" complete with its accompanying war on drugs. The reason drug cartels exist is because of *money*. However, in reality, this is only symptomatic of the problem. While we should always follow the money, we need to go back even further to the indistinct figure deeply hidden in the unfathomable recesses of the shadows. At the root of *all* crime, there is *Satan*. At the root of all immorality, there is *Satan*.

Wherever there is avarice, unchecked greed, and a desire for ill-gotten wealth, there is *Satan*.

In short, Satanism is anything that is *anti-God*. The strategies that Satan has utilized over the years are not revealed in one vice. Satan has covered the gamut, so that all people, from all lifestyles have an opportunity to follow him (ultimately worshiping him) with a method and lifestyle that suits that person. While of course, not everyone prefers to approach Satan with bloodied animal or human in hand, there are any numbers of ways to follow Satan without even realizing it.

It is important that people – *especially authentic Christians* – come to understand that long ago, Satan crafted a plan, a *thorough*, *multi-faceted* plan that provides something for *everyone*. He did not put all of his evil intentions in one basket.

This plan, created and put into effect by Satan and all those fallen entities and Nephilim under him, is meant to capture *all of humanity*. The subject of all these chapters together makes up a large portion of Satan's plan. Certainly though, this book does not cover everything. The charts at the end of this book focus mainly on areas within the *New Age Movement*, which is overwhelmingly large in itself.

Over the years, the public has been told a good many things about Satanism and how it does not really exist as first believed. People like Warnke, Stratford, Brown, Michaelsen, and many others were charged with making it up because they wanted nothing more than to cash in on the panic they set in motion.

There is something wrong with the picture we have been presented by those who have *opposed* the people who have attempted to warn the world about Satanism. What may be wrong with it is what has been deliberately *hidden* from the public. However, roughly forty years later, in the middle of 2010, it has become too widespread to ignore any longer.

Satan is *THE* Source

People have been harassed, discredited, and lives have been lost in the process of trying to bring much of this type of information to light. Sadly, Christians have become the new breed of *witch hunters* against other Christians, and the world applauds, while so-called investigative journalists pat themselves on their backs.

There is a *source* at work. That source stands against God, all people, and certainly against all authentic believers. Is it possible for Satan to *use* authentic believers? Of course, as the case of Peter shows, when he told Christ that He would never be killed and Christ said, *"Get the behind me, **SATAN**!"* (cf. Matthew 16:23). Anyone can be used of Satan, Christian or not.

Did Satan use people in the 1970s, 80s, and 90s to downplay the idea that a network of people exists who worship him, doing so by committing atrociously horrible acts of violence? It is very possible.

The whole thing is reminiscent of "The X-Files" TV show, in which Agent Mulder is routinely *not* believed by nearly everyone he works with regarding the existence of *aliens*. Scully *wants* to believe him, but even she has a difficult time with it; however, the truth is out there, so Mulder keeps pursuing it.

Like X-Files, the truth about Satanism and those who worship him *is out there* and once again, coming to the fore. Are you really interested in knowing the truth, or is it something you cannot handle?

2

SATANISM
EVER-WIDENING GAP

It is this author's belief that we are seeing an interesting and *revealing* phenomenon at work today throughout society and the Visible Church. Years ago, it was not nearly as noticeable, but today it is becoming exceedingly apparent. Apart from the obvious signs of Satanism gaining notice, something else is happening.

What we are seeing is a *gap* beginning to appear between those who are the *Tares* and those who are *Wheat*. In other words, within the Visible Church are people who are both authentic Christians and those who only *profess* to be. Within the latter group, there are individuals who *will* become authentic Christians. Mixed in with them are those who will *never* become true Christians. Years ago, because of the norms of society, people kept things to themselves. Only those people who really knew someone knew what they were like and at times, not even then. There existed a sense of propriety that has gone the way of the dinosaur from our society today.

Trash Talk
Think about what the average person hears or sees on a daily basis. There is little need for people to actually watch what they say in their speech. The "F" word has become widely accepted as a valuable word because of its ability to express concepts without the person actually having to say what is literally meant.

The "F" word is the perfect substitute for a noun, an adjective, an adverb, and numerous other parts of speech. Because of it, no one really needs to *think* today. There is no reason to expand the vocabulary because the "F" word is always there to be used any way it needs to be used. A good example is when someone says, "F**k, the F**kin' F**kers. There is one definitive article in that sentence, with the "F" word as a verb, an adjective, and a noun.

Coupled with this verbal assault on our ears, attitudes of people have changed. Society has generally grown greedier, less content, and more people stand there with their hands out, and a "don't tell me what to do" position that flies in the face of respect and decency. If people thought chivalry died sometime ago, then we can only assume it has finally been buried.

It is not uncommon to ask someone to turn their music down (even when asked politely) to receive anything from a death stare, to a verbal retaliation, to someone pretending they did not hear the request. No one anymore likes to be told what to do because it is *inconvenient* and it means that if they acquiesce, they may be seen as a slave or servant instead of a person who has free will to choose. This will not do, so people resist all attempts to by others to make them do things they do not want to do.

Here in California, it is against the law to use a cell phone in a vehicle without using a hands free earpiece or device. That does not matter, because one can quickly lose count of how many people ignore this law, which was enacted for reasons of *safety*. It was not that long ago while driving on one of the major highways, I noticed a car in front of me (in the fast lane) that was going slower than the rest of the traffic. That is not unusual because a great deal of people believe that if they are going the speed limit, they do not have to move out of the way for faster cars coming up behind them. While this may be the legal aspect of that law, it simply makes good sense (and good manners) to pull over and let those who want to speed go on their way. It also reduces the chance of road rage as well. There again, people do not move over simply because they are *self-centered*.

Selfishness Is as Selfishness Does
At any rate, there were two people in the car ahead of me, and it was difficult to not notice their heads bobbing up and down. Quickly realizing that they may both have been texting, I changed lanes and pulled up next to them. Glancing over, I could see that both men in the car (one driver and one passenger) were *both* busy texting. It did not matter to them whether or not their car was going slower, or that the driver was having a difficult time keeping his car in his lane. What mattered was that they both had something to say and now was the time to say it. Obviously, the passenger is excused, but not the driver.

I beeped my horn, they both looked over, and I made a sign of driving. Instead of flipping me off, to his credit, the driver stopped texting and actually started driving. I am not sure how long he did this, but at least he did it. His reaction is an anomaly because most could care less about anyone else on the word. It does not matter if it is changing lanes without using blinkers (also against the law), or texting while driving, or talking on the cell phone without using a hands free device, people prefer to do what is best only for themselves and too bad for everyone else.

Now because someone breaks these driving laws does not mean that they are a Tare. However, this symptom of a society stems *from* Tares who are beginning to make their presence felt.

Tares are now more clearly seen for the type of *religious* worship they are involved in. Will you see Tares involved in outright worship of the devil? Probably not, though it certainly could happen. What is more likely instead is that Tares will be part of the *Emergent Church*, which does a number of things:

- *Questions the authority of the Bible*
- *Questions salvation and the means by which people receive it*
- *Questions God, His Son, and the modus operandi of the Holy Spirit in and through the Invisible Church*
- *Preaches little, questions a lot*

Mystically Emergent Satanism
The Emergent Church is rife with mysticism and a feel-good mentality. Leaders of the Emergent Church stress how much God loves all people, in spite of their sexual proclivities, or other problems they face. There is no real need to change any of it, because God made people as they exist in this world. People should be free to express themselves and find God on their own terms.

The Emergent Church is nothing more than a thinly disguised "good" version of Satanism. It ties in very nicely with the New Age Movement and its emphasis on mysticism along with the belief that we are all gods. We merely need to find the way to self-actualize and that way may be different for every person. All paths lead to God and those who cannot fall in line with that thinking need to be quelled because their "hate" speech that there is only one way to God and that is through Jesus Christ is too narrow, too non-conformist, too anti-God to be real.

Tares Are Becoming Noticeable
Because of the Emergent Church especially, those individuals who are the Tares within the Visible Church now have a way to simply be themselves while still maintaining more than a modicum of religiosity. They can continue to be *religious*, while most of the world thinks that they are Christian because they attend Christian-type churches, or because they talk about God or the Bible, or even quote verses from the Bible. Of course, the sermons (if they can be called that), at many of these churches are the furthest thing from the actual gospel of Jesus Christ.

As time marches onward, it seems only natural that the Tares will become more obvious to authentic believers. Their true natures will be more readily visible along with the deception that they live under.

No authentic Christian is free from sin. All of us stumble, sin, and fall at times throughout our lives. This though pales in comparison to the amount and level of sin that Tares commit. These sins and failures give the Invisible Church a bad name because they bring dishonor to Jesus Christ.

While atheists and others may use the excuse that the church is filled with hypocrites as a reason to believe that there is no real value or veracity within the Invisible Church, all they are doing is proving what Jesus said about the type of person who comes to Him for salvation. All of us are failures. All of us are sinners. All of us need salvation because our "righteousness" simply does not cut it. It falls exceedingly short.

To say that the church has no integrity because of the people in it is the thinnest of excuses. The reality and integrity of the Church does not lie in the people who claim to be part of it. The reality and integrity of the Church rests solely in the One who formed it (and continues to form it), and that is Jesus Christ.

No one has an excuse to sin that God will accept. We sin because we are sinners. We sin as Christians because the sin nature remains with us. Jesus did not eradicate the sin nature when we received salvation through the new birth. It remains with us, in our flesh, constantly working against what God is doing in us.

Tares Do Not Equal Wheat
The Tares will never be authentic Christians, yet they will continue to *pretend* they are, all the while convincing others that the world is a far better place to be than the hypocritical environment of the Church. Through that belief, people believe God will let them off the hook. It will not happen and down deep, they know it to be true.

As we run headlong into the time of the Tribulation, the gap between the Tares and the Wheat will only increase. Persecution will become greater and the Tares will not want to have to deal with that, so they will go along with the program, offering one excuse after another for their *apostasy* from Christianity, while still calling themselves Christian.

Today, we are seeing more and more individuals walk away from Christianity. This is happening in droves. Many of those individuals who may have spent years involved in the church, come to a point of leaving. They often refer to themselves as *ex-Christians* and do not like it when someone points out that they could not have been authentic Christians.

What those people really did was simply *play* at Christianity because to them it was a *lifestyle*, like being a practicing Buddhist. One day, they woke up, no longer believed that it worked, so they left. This is what someone can do with a *lifestyle*. According to Scripture, it is *impossible* to walk away from something that Jesus refers to as the birth from above, or new birth (cf. John 3). This is a spiritual transaction, accomplished by God alone. It is also *permanent*. There is no going back, in spite of what many today think and teach today.

Exodus Will Continue
What we are seeing in the continued exodus from Christianity, is what the apostle Paul called the "great apostasy," (2 Thessalonians 2:1-3). In that passage, Paul explains some of the things that must come before the "day of the Lord" and one of them is the great apostasy. In simple terms, what this means is that people will be seen to walk away from the faith. They will actively choose to no longer be *involved* in Christianity.

While it may appear on the outside that people will be renouncing the faith of Christianity, what it actually means is that they will no longer continue the *practice* of being Christians *outwardly*. For all intents and purposes, the world will view this as Christians becoming non-Christian. Since they never really had the new birth though, they cannot actually walk away from being an authentic Christian. They will walk away from all *external* observances of what people *think* it means to be a Christian.

Those people will stop going to church. They will stop reading (and may even toss out) their Bibles. They will adopt another lifestyle altogether, possibly atheism, or agnosticism, or participate in aspects of the New Age Movement because at least there, all roads lead to god.

If Christ warned that from the beginning the enemy would sow Tares in Christ's Church, it is only natural to conclude that toward the end, when the going gets tough, the Tares will toss in the towel. Their lives were built on a lie anyway, and they will finally acknowledge what they have always believed, that *Christianity is not the way*. This will cause them to completely sever ties with all aspects of Christianity. Beyond this, they will also join in with others who are staunch in their opposition *to* Christianity. It has been this author's experience that people whom without equivocation, walk away from Christianity, end up becoming some of the most ardent opponents of it.

SATANISM
BELIEVING THE LIE

A minister told his congregation, "*Next week I plan to preach about the sin of lying. To help you understand my sermon, I want you all to read Mark 17.*"

The following Sunday, as he prepared to deliver his sermon, the minister asked for a show of hands. He wanted to know how many had read Mark 17. Every hand went up. The minister smiled and said, "*Mark has only sixteen chapters. I will now proceed with my sermon on the sin of lying.*"[24] We laugh at jokes like that (or at least chuckle) because we all know what it is like to be caught lying. It is embarrass-

---

[24] http://jokes4all.net/lying.html

ing and it often brings out the defensive nature in people. No one likes to be caught telling a lie.

Debunking the Truth?
When Satanism was becoming known back in the late 70s and early 80s, a number of individuals like those mentioned in the first chapter rose up to debunk it. They accomplished their purpose and because of it, the rise of Satanism sunk back into the recesses of oblivion, at least as far as the average person was concerned. No one wanted to be accused of being a lunatic by believing in horned red creatures with pitchforks and people bowing to them!

As mentioned, Cornerstone Magazine was the main publication that decided to deal with people they considered "tale bearers," or liars. We noted that Cornerstone Magazine, an offshoot of Jesus People USA, had its own brand of credibility problems if not directly, through connection with JPUSA.

Over the years since that time, things have changed and even quieted down quite a bit. However, we are now seeing a burgeoning growth of accusations of Satanism throughout the globe and this time it will be very difficult for Jon Trott, the Passantinos or anyone else to do what they did to bury the subject in the 1970s and 80s.

We will get back to Satanism in a moment, but first it might be good to look at JPUSA and Cornerstone because even though the magazine went out of business years ago, Jon Trot is still around, and a festival that began under the auspices of the two groups called, *Cornerstone Festival* continues to this day. Beginning in 1984, the festival started up in Grayslake, Illinois and from 1991 to present, the festival is held in Bushnell, Illinois. Years ago, a band known as Resurrection Band was the main headlining act, even before the festival started. They were a cross between southern rock and heavy metal, with a lead singer who could belt out a tune with the best of them.

The Mysticism of the C-Stone Festival

Regardless of how Cornerstone Festival (or C-Stone) began and with what intentions, it is clear that some questions need to be asked now. Dr. Gregory Reid comments on this year's line-up of seminars. *"This year at the famous Cornerstone Festival, which sees tens of thousands of Christian teens come through their gates, hear their bands and attend their 'workshops', looked like a full-on pagan festival this year. In addition to the full gaggle of new age friendly classes and bands that consistently flashed the 'hail satan' sign (the sign most of them mistakenly think means 'rock on'), there was a labyrinth, (In Greek mythology, the Labyrinth was an elaborate structure constructed for King Minos of Crete and designed by the legendary artificer Daedalus to hold the Minotaur, a creature that was half man and half bull) a kissing booth (for donations) a shirtless guy with 'free hugs' written on his body (would you want your teenage girl being hugged by a half naked stranger?) and classes such as:*

- *Being holistic*
- *Celtic monasticism*
- *The secret of homosexuality must be explored*
- *Literature of the oppressed: American women authors*
- *Native American Flute*
- *Rape Culture: Heirarchy and Violence*
- *Songs and stories from Native America"*[25]

What is interesting (if not scary), is the fact that there is much associated with the C-Stone Festival that smacks of *Satanism*! Gee, should that be a surprise? Reid continues by pointing out, *"'Imaginarium', the late Bob Passantino's 'favorite' Cornerstone exhibit: it truly was the 'cornerstone' of this years' festival. This year, they called it 'Days of the Dead,' and the web ad had a 'deadhead' type skeleton with a flower hat. Here's their own intro:*

---

[25] http://www.gregoryreid.com/id185.htm

'Keep the Hallow in Halloween! (aka Saints Preserve Us!) The 2006 Imaginarium at Cornerstone Festival honors Saints, Souls (and Bodies) in a series of Feasts of the Dead — from Dia de los Muertos to the Celtic harvest revels (did you catch that? They were celebrating DRUID FESTIVALS at a CHRISTIAN FESTIVAL! - GR) that became All Hallows' Eve. We'll also explore the darkest heart of the hit TV series LOST, survey the stylish and subtle horror films of Val Lewton, (re)acquaint ourselves with Dr. Who, and dig deep into the science, politics and even poetics of archaeology. Indeed, the imperial ruins of time and the grinning skulls of the feasts of the dead have much in common: human history has its own cycles of life and death —a continual reduction to rubble, a continual digging out. This year's Imaginarium explores both ends of that spectrum, reflecting on the transience of the City of Man and the more lasting legacy of citizens of the City of God. We've long claimed for our patron saint, G. K. Chesterton — and St. Gilbert may well have claimed for his own, Francis, that 'jester of God.' As a part of our All Saints focus, we'll examine what it means to be a saint, with a special emphasis on the Poor Man of Assisi. Our aim is to get beyond the popular sentimentalization of the saint and recover what it means to be such a 'knight of faith.' We'll also pay our respects to St. Leibowitz, the centerpiece of a classic science fiction novel which makes an unforgettable survey of history and humanity within it."[26]

Apparently, the C-Stone Festival celebrated what turns out to be the "Day of the Dead" with specific displays that included a skeleton in a coffin among other things. Apparently, in Mexico, this is called *"Dia de los Muertos,"* and is nothing but an occult celebration of the dead! One must ask, why is *this* event being celebrated at an event that is allegedly Christian in nature?

Dr. Reid finishes his commentary on the C-Stone Festival by making several pertinent points and asking some hard questions?

---

[26] http://www.gregoryreid.com/id185.htm

"Welcome to Babylon, folks. You were warned in the eighties, and then the nineties - if you don't WAKE UP and stop the infiltration of occultists and occultism in the church, it would get worse and we would be sacrificing a whole generation of kids to its gods. We are there. As one who was exposed to pagan festivals growing up and seen many since, I challenge anyone to show me how this was any different than any other wiccan/satanic/pagan celebration. In fact, any wiccan or satanist or pagan would feel right at home here, and in fact would not see it as "Christian" at all.

"I challenge Hank Hanegraff of Christian Research Institute to explain how he can support Gretchen Passantino in the light of these clearly occult-friendly activities and philosophies. What about it, Hank? Get off the fence or throw in your hat with this Bacchus-loving crowd.

"I challenge Gretchen Passantino to answer the question I posed to her and Bob by phone years ago: ARE YOU A WICCAN? Because, you know, if it walks and quacks like a duck...

"And one more question to all of them: WHY should we believe a single word you wrote about the occult "satanic panic" in the 1990's when it is now so evident where your religious leanings and loyalties lie - not with Biblical Christianity that forbids all things occult, but with pagan-friendly philosophies, teachings and outreaches?

"I can only hope they continue to come out of the occult closet so we can see who they really are, and maybe people will stop sending their kids to get "passed through the fire" of the Cornerstone occult festivals.

"Welcome to the Emerging Church, folks. Gregory Reid"[27]

The Assault on the Church

What we are seeing is nothing less than a massive assault on the Invisible Church and authentic believers. It would appear that many

---

[27] http://www.gregoryreid.com/id185.htm

within the Christian community might very well be behind some of the cover-up that has occurred over the years. The other part of this equation is that it appears that Satan is attempting to convince the entire world that all of these things are connected by the same common denominator and there is absolutely nothing wrong with that denominator. In other words, he is working out his plan to cause people to believe that all roads lead to the same god, so it does not matter what road a person happens to be on.

It may be that Satan was not ready to have his hidden agenda made public thirty years or more ago, and used people (knowingly or unknowingly) to help push that truth back down and out of sight, into the hidden recesses of darkness. It is tragic that individuals' lives were discredited and the absolute vengefulness and spite that came from the Satanic "debunkers" really speaks for itself.

Now in 2010, it appears as if it does not matter if either society or the church knows about the satanically inspired proclivities of many. It is almost as if Satan believes it is too late to do anything about it. The truth though is that God is fully in control and has always been in control. What comes to the surface does so because of His sovereignty and does not depend upon Satan, his fallen angels or people.

What we see taking place is the coming together of a myriad of avenues – all seemingly *unique* and *unrelated* – coming together as *one*, all of it emanating from one central *hub*. By the time it reaches the outer edge of the wheel, it has morphed into something else, but with the same inner core as all the rest of the spokes. Within the Visible Church, we have seen what has become known as the Emergent Church and we are aware of the damage it is causing. Orthodox doctrine is going out the door, replaced with mysticism and doctrines of demons.

The interesting thing is that during the day of the Charismatic Movement, though people may deny it, it was (and remains) based on *feeling* and is therefore *mystical* in nature. People claimed to have "heard" directly from God. They were inspired to do things that were contrary to Scripture, but since they *felt* or *believed* that these inspirations were from God, then how could they be wrong?

God Loves Everybody!

People long to feel good about themselves and life. They want to be happy, filled with joy, entering into a mystical or ethereal relationship with God. Because He *is* God, then a relationship with Him *should* be mystical, it is believed. This line of thinking almost always opens people up to error and deception. It may not start out that way, but once the enemy can successfully turn people away from the Bible by focusing on their feelings, then he can eventually cause them to doubt the veracity of Scripture entirely. This leaves them with only one course of action in determining truth, and that is *subjectivism*. People become their highest authority and *they* determine if something is right or wrong, strictly by how they *feel* about it. If it *seems* to stray from Scripture, that does not matter because they firmly believe that God has spoken to them and because of it, they *must* obey.

It has become clear to all but those who are blind and deaf that something is going on that has become the undergirding of society throughout the world for generations. Something evil is afoot and apparently, that evil now believes it to be safe enough to, once again rise to the surface, this time under its own power and with no qualms and no roadblocks.

This time, naysayers are non-existent because many of them are actually *involved* in some aspect of this demonically inspired cultural shift. As far as they are concerned, there is nothing to debunk and discredit. It is simply the natural progression and evolution of the church in this sphere. Their god is speaking and they are listening.

Even in its rising awareness, people will not see it for what it is, preferring instead to believe that it is simply another cultural norm, or simply an offshoot of certain aspects of society. It will be seen as another way that people express themselves and they should be allowed to express who they are without fear of reprisal, or put down.

From Horror to Paranormal
What has changed since the 1970s is that horror movies have become much more infused with the paranormal. Rock music has gone from "*Dancing in the Moonlight*" to *sacrificing* in the moonlight. Everywhere you look, pentagrams and satanic symbolism and imagery abounds. It is taken for granted and it has literally become part of society.

Because of this, in many ways Satanism seems to have been *declawed*. There is no longer fear of it because it is merely a fad, something that will go away or change into something else over time and once that happens, then something new will take its place.

Satan is not an idiot. He is extremely powerful. I say that only out of respect for the amount of power God continues to allow him to have, but I do not say that for any other reason. I do not respect *him*, I only respect what he has the power to *accomplish*.

If not for God's protection, Satan would have a field day with all authentic believers, torturing us, making our lives miserable in some other way, or killing us outright. I do not kid myself that his power to destroy is so far above anything on this earth. Yet, I also understand that it is God who protects me constantly and even *if* God were to allow Satan to physically harm me (as he did to Job in the OT), there is absolutely *nothing* that Satan can do to my soul, which rests securely in God's hands.

In the 1970s and 80s, Satanism was becoming known through people like Warnke, Stratford, and Brown. Others also came forward, but as soon as their credibility was questioned and destroyed, the air went completely out of the entire situation.

Satan obviously knew another time would come (*had* to come) in which his work and the work of his *human* followers would rise to the surface simply because of the immense number of people involved in it. Because of that, he went on the *offensive*. Instead of raising people up to *discredit* others, as he seems to have done in the past, he did something far better. He has spent years becoming the butt of his own jokes. He has *parodied* himself and in the process has established himself as someone that is not to be feared. Satan, his symbols, his mode of operation, and his work have become so well known through movies, music, and books that people no longer panic at the mention of his name. Satan has succeeded in making himself a joke, not to be taken seriously and certainly, not to be feared.

People routinely go to rock concerts in which Satan is glorified through pentagrams and other satanic symbolism. The lead singers of these bands belt out songs glorifying Satan and his work. Teenagers by the millions attend these concerts, buy the CDs, the shirts, and other paraphernalia all because it is the *in* thing and they are drawn to it. They honestly believe that *if* the Dark Lord exists, he exists to make human beings *happy* and he has simply gotten a bad rap by "fundamental" Christians from generations past.

Hollywood Glorifies Satan
The concept of true evil has either been emasculated by Hollywood and everything that comes out of it, or it has been made so evil that no one believes that type of evil could actually exist. Evil, in many instances, is no different from good; it is merely in how a person *perceives* it or uses it that makes it good or evil.

In 2010, good angels are seen as bad ("The Fallen," or "Legion"), and bad angels (often represented by sorcery, aka the Harry Potter series), are seen as *good*. Hollywood, under Satan's careful direction has taught the buying public that life is what you make it and what may appear to be good, might in reality be bad, and vice versa.

Where will it end and why is this happening? It will end when God Almighty brings it to an end. It is happening because we are living in the Last Days and the entire world is gearing up for the one huge war that Satan hopes to win against the God of the universe.

In order to accomplish his task, Satan essentially needs to *convert* the entire world to his way of thinking. The people of earth need to be turned literally, to the dark side, all the while believing that the dark side is the *good* side, the only side. Those who do not *turn* or *convert* will be dealt with accordingly and things are already being put in place to ensure that the malcontents, the dissenters will be removed from society.

Satan is accomplishing his goal and God is allowing it because ultimately, God will show the entire world and universe that *no one* stands before Him, nor is anyone His equal (including Satan). God will prove that He and He alone is Victor *without* equal, intimidated by no one and defeated by none. God is Victor now and forever, amen.

Satan: Something to Laugh At and Nothing to Fear
So what has Satan been doing that has caused people to relax their fears toward him? How has he managed to turn himself into an ongoing joke so that people will smile, smirk, or laugh at the mention of Satan? Those who do not find Satan funny are coming round to believe that *they* can control *him* with the use of spells, incantations, and ritual sacrifices. They believe that by following the prescribed directives of ancient religions, Satan and his multitude of fallen angels have no choice but to do man's bidding.

What are the specific avenues in which Satan has worked and continues to work in order to walk his goals and purposes into fruition right through the front door?

He has done it the way he has always done it, by *mixing truth* with *lies*. He has created situations in which people have modified their view of Satan, satanic ritualism, and associated crime so that they come to believe the lie he presents. Because they believe the lie (and Satan himself **seems** to be bound by it), they are *mollified*. These people have come to believe that Satan is nothing to fear, because he is merely a *being* with power who wants to share his power with humanity, something that God does *not* want to do.

For those who do not believe there is a being known as Satan, he is simply a dark impersonal force that all one needs to do is tap into and in doing so, will gain immeasurable success, enlightenment, and satisfaction.

Satan has covered all of his bases and for every individual on this planet, he has provided a way for them to accept either him, or the *idea* of him. In this way, people have slowly and consistently moved to his side of the equation, believing it to be the only real, pragmatic option available.

The Bible tells us that in the *end times*, God sends a delusion so that people will believe *the* lie (2 Thessalonians 2:11). People have long argued about the lie and what in contains. This author believes that *the lie* is everything that Satan uses to deceive people on this planet. Everything. He holds nothing back, tossing everything into the mix so that there will be and is something for every person alive.

For those who are not interested in truth, preferring to believe lies, God will *give them over to it*, as the apostle Paul notes in his letter to the Thessalonians. Are you one who prefers the lie? Do you believe that what is happening today in our society is nothing with which to be concerned? If so, please read on, as it may make a difference in your worldview.

SATANISM
ILLUMINATI & FREEMASONRY

It is generally known that Adam Weishaupt is the founder of the Illuminati. From his goals and objectives, a plan was put into motion that would come to include the world's most powerful elite. The essential overall goal of this organization was to "*further each other's goals at the expense of others and under a shroud of secrecy.*"[28]

From humble beginnings came the egotistical leanings of one man who garnered the attention, interest, and loyalty of *many* men

---

[28] Mark Dice *The Illuminati Facts & Fiction* (The Resistance, 2009), 5

throughout the world. They have been planning world domination since their beginnings and have come a long way in bringing that one goal to fruition.

Obviously, for a group such as the Illuminati to survive, a number of things have to be built into it:

- Complete loyalty to one another within the group
- Absolute secrecy on pain of death
- Numerous branches of the Illuminati like "Skull & Bones," etc. so that the group can become truly *global*
- The one main goal broken down into smaller "bites" so that the overall goal could come to fruition in segments
    - Infiltrate and govern all mainstream media outlets
    - Infiltrate and hold sway over what Hollywood produces in movies and television
    - Gain control of the music industry

Illuminati Organization
Mark Dice, in his book *The Illuminati Facts & Fiction*, points out that Joe Valachi became the insider of the Italian Mafia who released pertinent information about this criminal family. Initially not believed, he was placed in a mental institution.

Only later, when what Valachi had shared with authorities about the fact that the Mafia had judges, politicians and other law enforcement officials in their pockets, did officials realize that Valachi had been telling them the truth.

In many ways, by understanding how the mob works, we see a microcosm for the Illuminati. The mob works because they are able to grease or payoff people in high-ranking positions, whether they are police officers, judges, politicians, or whomever, the idea that everyone has a price turns out to be true. Those who did not have a price and therefore could not be bought were often fitted with concrete shoes.

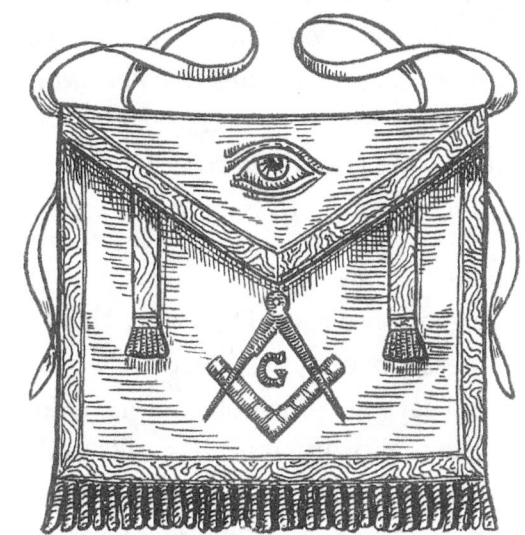

The Illuminati works this way as well, except the difference is that the people in these high-ranking positions – bankers, CEOs, politicians, and more – are *in* the Illuminati. Because they are part of the Illuminati, it is merely a matter of getting things done at their level, so that other things can be done at lower levels. Think of it. If the Illuminati controls most or all of the mainstream media, then they have access to virtually all the information that they release to the public. Not only that, but they can *create* the information that is disseminated to the public. In general, the public will have no clue whether what they are hearing or reading is true or false. This is the power that dwells *within,* and emanates, *from* the Illuminati.

Anyone who controls information and access to it truly has the highest form of power on earth, among human beings at least. This control removes any power from the common individual. Only those individuals, who find out something, either inadvertently or otherwise, are inclined to look further to see where the trail ends. Many of these people, as many books and documents have pointed out, have disappeared, or wound up dead. Coincidence?

What is more than interesting about the Illuminati is what they ultimately believe will happen *after* they gain control of the world. *"New Age and occult teachings predict that when the New World Order infrastructure and ideologies are complete, that from within the hierarchy of the Illuminati will arrive the long awaited messiah. They be-*

lieve that he will unite all the world's religions into one compatible formula, and that he will fulfill all prophecies of the coming world savior. They also say that at this time the secret hierarchy of enlightened masters will then be able to come out from the shadows in what is called the externalization of the hierarchy, and then finally show themselves to the world and reveal the hidden wisdom that they had kept sheltered for countless generations."[29]

Peace at Last?
Dice goes onto reveal that once this New Age messiah is here, all sickness, poverty, prejudice and crime will become a thing of the past. Peace and harmony among the world's citizens will finally become a reality and it is all thanks to the Illuminati, who knew it all along, but needed to remain in secret to protect the common people from one another. Working secretly also protected those within the Illuminati from those who would naturally come against them.

Because the messiah will have finally stepped out from among them, they can reveal who they are without fear of any negative consequences to them. Those within the Illuminati actually believe that the messiah, who comes from within their ranks, will be *"some kind of super-human demigod or even a being from another planet or dimension."*[30]

Of course, these are the beliefs of those within the New Age Movement, the occult, and the Illuminati, which is why these people often attend *church*. To them, it is not a problem since they believe themselves to be "Christians." In fact, they believe themselves to be *superior* to Christians because they believe they have discovered the hidden knowledge that Christians and others only wish they knew. This same mentality exists within the New Age Movement, with the clicking of their tongues, and shaking of their heads, looking mournfully

---
[29] Mark Dice *The Illuminati Facts & Fiction* (The Resistance, 2009), 11
[30] Ibid, 12

at the narrow-minded Christian who has not yet come to self-actualization with the truth.

Christians, on the other hand understand the above-described scenario quite a bit differently. Though we believe that it will happen, that one individual will step out from among all the Illuminati, and will be hailed as the world's ultimate and final savior, in actuality, this individual will be none other than Antichrist, fully imbued with Satan's power and malevolence. Of course, that malevolence will remain hidden until the middle of the Tribulation when he breaks the covenant that he signed with Israel and other parties in the Middle East for peace. Once he breaks his promise, hell really has a field day! With only three and a half years left of the Tribulation before Christ returns, Antichrist has a great deal to accomplish in such a short time and draws on all of his supernatural strength from his father (Satan) to accomplish it.

"Just as Adolph Hitler promised peace and economic prosperity in Germany once the Jews were eliminated, the Antichrist will offer the same solution and single out the resistant Christians and others as the obstacle to peace and prosperity."[31]

Gone in a Twinkling of an Eye!
From what has been learned from other sources and already reported in other books written by this author, it is clear that currently within the New Age Movement is the teaching that at one point in the future, somewhere in the neighborhood of 20 million individuals will instantly disappear from the face of the earth. This information has been transmitted from those referred to as ascended or higher masters, or aliens from Pleiades, or Sirrius or somewhere else altogether for some time.

---

[31] Mark Dice *The Illuminati Facts & Fiction* (The Resistance, 2009), 12

Of course, the above information is setting the world up for a time when the Rapture *does* occur and millions are gone instantly. The explanation is that those who were holding the earth and its people back from developing to the next spiritual level will be removed.

In the case of Antichrist, when he gains power, he will obviously want to put into place, implanted chips within the body of every person. There are probably several reasons for that, but the obvious one has to do with a person being unable to buy or sell without this "mark."

Another reason may very well have to do with mind-control techniques that our government and other governments have been working on and perfecting for generations. The advances that have been made in mind-control, through electromagnetic frequencies alone is astounding (we will deal more with this further in this book).

For those who do not accept an implant, they will be viewed as traitors to the world. Because of that, they will of necessity need to be destroyed. It is those people who still believe that owning land, owning your own business, and living under the freedoms found within the U.S. Constitution is superior to living under a dictatorship, however peaceful it appears to be.

When the Antichrist gains full control of the world, there will be no room left for dissenters and those in power under the imperialistic dictatorship of Antichrist will quickly deal with them. The rest of the world will gladly fall in line behind Antichrist, believing him to be the last savior of the world and the one for which the world has been waiting.

Freemasonry
Freemasonry and the Illuminati go hand in hand. In fact, both share the same religious doctrine: *Luciferianism* or *Satanism*. There are really two main branches of Satanism; atheistic and theistic. Mark Dice

sums it up this way, "*Atheistic Satanism was popularized in the late 1960s by Anton LaVey, the founder of the Church of Satan and the author of The Satanic Bible. While misleading and confusing, he and his followers profess that they are atheists and don't believe in a literal Devil, or even God. They don't believe in an afterlife or a Heaven or Hell, either. These individuals choose to call themselves Satanists and use the symbol of Satan for its rebellious and nonconformist connotations.*"[32]

So to be a Satanist after the order of LaVey, one merely has to be an atheist. "*Theistic Satanism, on the other hand, is the belief in a God and a Devil, and supernatural beings. These Satanists take the opposite side of the Christian view concerning the Garden of Eden and the Fall of Man. In Judaism and Christianity, the book of Genesis describes how God created Adam and Eve and how they lived in the Garden of Eden. God was said to have told them that they were not to eat the forbidden fruit from the tree of knowledge of good and evil, for if they did, they would surely die.*"[33] Dice then goes onto relate the rest of the narrative in which Satan in the form of a serpent convinces Eve that God is simply being selfish. He does not want Eve or Adam to have this *insider* knowledge.

"*Theistic Satanist and Luciferians believe that Satan came to the Garden of Eden to save Adam and Eve and mankind from ignorance, and that God didn't want them to have the knowledge because then they wouldn't be his slaves. In this view, God is seen as the oppressor and the evil one, and Satan is seen as the hero and savior. This is why in such books as* The Secret Doctrine, *author Helena Blavatsky calls Satan the holy spirit.*"[34]

---

[32] Mark Dice *The Illuminati Face & Fiction* (The Resistance, 2009), 17
[33] Ibid, 17
[34] Ibid, 18

Because the members of the Illuminati believe that they have the truth, which has been hidden for generations, the knowledge that they *do* have is only disseminated to members little by little. As an individual goes higher in rank within the Illuminati, they become entitled to learn more of the hidden knowledge.

Dice also rightly points out that the name "Lucifer" means "light bearer" and it is because of this, Theistic Satanists and Luciferians believe Satan is the *true* source of light, not Jesus Christ. This is at least in part why those who think like this often become angry or even irate when hearing Christians speak of Jesus as *the Light.* In the view of Satanists/Luciferians, Christians are taking what belongs to Satan and attributing it to Jesus, which they believe to be wrong.

Dice also again rightly points out that while authentic Christians believe that salvation comes only through the *redemptive work of Jesus Christ*, Theistic Satanists, occultists, and Luciferians believe that true salvation comes only through awareness of the *hidden knowledge.* This hidden knowledge is believed to incorporate *far more* than can be found in the Person of Jesus Christ and the Bible. Believing that salvation comes only through Jesus Christ is narrow, divisive, and untrue (according to these groups).

It is because of this outlook and worldview Dice explains, that those within the Illuminati are able to justify themselves when they commit all manner of crimes, like murder, thievery, or even mind-control on people who have no idea they are guinea pigs. People who believe that their salvation is found in this secret (or "occult") knowledge, also have no qualms about believing that they can use *any* means at their disposal to keep others from knowing about it, unless those people are invited into the inner circle.

It is because of this thinking and worldview that there exist two frames of reference with respect to the afterlife. Either these people believe that human beings are simply the top of the totem pole among all life, but still animals. In that sense then, there is no existence after this life. The other belief is in line with many of the ancient civilizations such as Ancient Egypt, in which a person's deeds are weighed – good against bad – and the side that weighs the most determines the ultimate destination of the person, or whether they must come back to be reincarnated again.

This is exactly why people like Adolph Hitler became convinced that he was an authentic Christian. He had the secret knowledge and it is a well-known fact that he did more than dabble in the occult. He believed that he was doing the world *and God* a huge favor by eliminating the people (Jews) who had killed Jesus. Even though to Hitler, Jesus was not *the* God, He was nonetheless a very important prophet.

Of course, what Hitler and others constantly miss is that Jews were not the only ones who put Jesus to death. Both Jews *and* Gentiles had a hand in it. Pontius Pilate – a Gentile – could have and should have released Jesus because he found nothing wrong with Him. Roman soldiers who scourged Jesus unmercifully and then nailed His hands and feet to the cross also bear the responsibility.

In other words, all people had a hand in killing Jesus and all of us bear the guilt of that act. However, in His infinite love, mercy, and wisdom, His death also serves to release us from our captivity to Satan, allowing us the opportunity to *choose* to serve Jesus Christ. That is salvation because it begins in this life and completes in the next.

SATANISM
ENTERTAINMENT

There can be no argument that Satan and his subordinates rule the air *and* this earth. Of course, this takes place under the watchful eye of God Almighty, yet God has continued to allow the prince of this world to do things as if his fate has not been sealed. The simple reason for this is to bring all things to fruition with God as ultimate Conqueror. One day, when the timing is perfect, God will physically vanquish this foe of foes. In the meantime, it is important to understand that God has allowed Satan to rule this planet as if he owns it and will always own it.

All Part of the Plan
Because of that, Satan works to bring his plans to completion. We know that he has an unnumbered host of fallen angels, demons, and Nephilim at his service and since he cannot be everywhere at once, they aids him tremendously in bringing his goals to their hoped for result.

While Satan knows (as do the fallen angels, demons, and Nephilim), his end is sure, he works as if that end *does not exist*. In truth, he has no other choice. He certainly cannot give up, or throw in the towel, and so he does what anyone in his position would do, pushes forward hoping beyond hope that he will actually have a chance of defeating God Almighty. There is no chance, but we need to understand that we are in the *now* and because of that, we are affected by what he does now, as God permits.

It is also helpful to understand something about Satan. It is necessary to comprehend *how* he has worked and *how* he has created a strong foundation of evil that has ultimately permeated society at every level. We have stated this before in other books, but the truth of the matter is that <u>everything</u> he does, <u>everything</u> he builds, and <u>everything</u> he causes people to believe comes under the heading of "Satanism."

Worshiping Satan is not the only thing that *creates* Satanism. There are certainly those who do that. While not as overt as directly worshiping him, everything that Satan has given rise to is, in some form or another, *Satanism*. There can be no argument here because he is completely *anti-God*. All things that flow from him then, by their very nature are also *anti-God*. Consequently, every individual who involves himself or herself in any aspect of life that is *anti-God* is by that very nature, following the prince of darkness. Simply because there are those who have come to the fore in years past and who believe they have successfully done the world a favor by putting to rest the allegedly ridiculous claims of a ex-Satanists, it does not mean that they have actually accomplished anything other than simply ruining a few lives. They could very well have squashed *truth*.

What these "investigative journalists" have only achieved is creating a shield by which Satan can continue his covert activities in all other areas of society, while allowing people to believe that this world is not as bad as some have testified. In essence, the people who have led the charge against certain individuals in the past have been themselves deceived and have then successfully deceived millions into believing their errant position that Satan would *never* be so crass as to have people worship him directly and with the shedding of blood in the process.

When the hidden ritualistic acts of ex-Satanists became known in the 1970s and 80s, I believe that subject was squelched for a number of reasons. Those reasons will should unfold as you read this book. The world was genuinely shocked and certain writers because of their own agenda felt it necessary to bury the idea of ritualistic killings deep underground.

Satan IS as Satan DOES

What people fail to see is that, as mentioned, *anything* and *everything* that pulls people away from the only God of the entire universe, is unequivocally *Satanic.* Satan can infest the arts, books, music, TV shows, movies, attitudes, beliefs and everything in between with *his* viewpoints. Because of that *everything* that is anti-God stems from Satan himself. Why is it difficult for some to believe that Satan does not care *how* people wind up worshiping him (directly or indirectly)? All that Satan cares about is that people *do* worship him.

For those who are into the macabre, the gothic, and the subject of death and dying, there are things that Satan has created that allow them to be who they are, while investing themselves in pagan activities. These people may not believe that Satan is real (though many do). They may believe in an impersonal force that one can tap into, in order to gain *strength*, *power*, and *enlightenment*.

Certainly, the fans who follow and listen to music by *Marilyn Manson*, Black Sabbath, Korn, and other death metal groups, have no qualms about enjoying the subjects found within his music. To them, this is merely an extension of their own personality that is naturally, where they feel most comfortable.

If we are going to condemn the credibility of Satanic Ritual Abuse (SRA) and killings because it *appears* too outlandish to be real in our modern times, and therefore unbelievable, then we need to do the same thing where rock music, TV, and movies are concerned. What is so difficult to believe about Satan being able to deceive the masses with things that cater to a person's likes and dislikes?

Yes, the one large difference is that *crimes* occur when people are ritually slaughtered in the name of Satan. However, as tragic and macabre as that is, there are people in this world who achieve an adrenalin rush from being involved in something like that. Some people in this world cannot get a rush like that unless they are diving off the world's highest precipice or manmade structure with only a small parachute, or by skiing down a mountain on one ski with an avalanche of snow following close on their heels.

There are records of criminals throughout history and into recent times, who were involved in some of the most heinous and unbelievable acts of massacre and slaughter ever recorded. Should we discount their crimes because we do not possess *all* the evidence, or because we did not see it with our own eyes?

It is *clear* that people are capable of thinking as these criminals think. It is abundantly clear as well that people are capable of *doing* what these individuals have done and many of them have shown absolutely no remorse at all when found caught, eventually found guilty, and even when subsequently put to death by the state. This should tell us something about how far down a human being could go.

Did Jeffrey Dahmer kill and dismember people as a boy? No, according to reports, he started with *animals*. Over time, he became more interested in pornography and then grew from a desire to kill animals, to killing and dismembering human beings. How does that *happen*? It can happen in any number of ways, but in any case, it usually takes place over *time*.

It Happens Over Time
People who become involved in outright and direct Satanic *worship*, involving ritual sacrifices of animals (and even humans), become involved through *stages*. No one wakes up one day and says, *"Today, I am going to become deeply immersed in Satanism. I want to see what it feels like to take the life of another person in a sacrificial setting in the hopes that I will gain tremendous power!"*

History is filled with people who have committed terrible crimes the world over (some of the most heinous during times of war between nations). They have often done so based on their belief in and their desire to please *Satan*. Charles Manson comes to mind. Richard Ramirez is another one. The aforementioned Jeffrey Dahmer is also included in this group, as is Hitler, on a grand scale.

Apart from this though, there have been many serial killers and rapists who were obviously *controlled* by Satan or one of his underlings. A normal human being could not have done what these people did to other people.

Ed Gein, a murderer and grave robber who cut up body pieces and made knick-knacks out of them is notorious for his crimes. Ted Bundy was a man who seemed to have had two personalities and could easily hide one only to let it out when he found a new victim.

Dennis Rader, the BTK killer, spent thirty years as a member of a local church, but also raped and killed many women and their family members. It was only due to his oversized ego that Rader was caught after years of no activity. He could not handle the fact that the case had become cold, and police had nothing to follow anymore, so he brought it to the surface again. What he failed to realize is that technology had gotten far better since the early days when he raped and killed. This time, using forensics software, he was tracked down, caught, tried, convicted, and in August 2005 was sentenced to ten consecutive life terms. Accordingly, he must serve 175 years before he even has a chance of being paroled. Rader has consistently shown no emotion or remorse for the slayings. He is a *stone*.

In a letter to police before he was caught, he *calmly* explained the process of the killings and how it was a huge sexual release for him. This author has read some of the transcripts and "without remorse" is an understatement. Rader also stated that he was *controlled* by the "x-factor" and only people who were also controlled by the same thing would understand what he was talking about. What was the x-factor? Who knows, but there is a good likelihood that though Rader did not recognize it as demonic possession, it was nothing else but possession. We will deal more with this subject later on in this book.

In previous books, we have presented some of the details of how Satan is bringing things about that will help his ambitions materialize. In fact, we have shown (as well as many other authors), that he has been at work for quite some time through a variety of people, from all walks of life, who have had a major impact on education, politics, and religion.

To sift through this labyrinth of people and their evil purposes is mindboggling and it is impossible for one book to cover all of it. However, it is clear that in this book, some groundwork needs to be enunciated. We noted in our previous chapters that Satan seemed to be almost undone when his work along with those who worship him started to become known in the 1970s and 80s. He seemingly worked hard and fast to squelch as much of it as possible and he was successful to a point.

Now, however, the time appears ripe for Satan to not only *allow* his foundational and underground work to come to the surface, but he may very well be *encouraging* it. If this is the case, then it would also appear that he believes he has things under control and that the people of the world are ready to receive him in whatever form he chooses to reveal himself. He has many disguises, though of course his favorite guise is the angel of light.

In the remaining chapters, we are going to take the time to invest ourselves with the awareness that comes from knowing the various avenues that have become part of the world's fabric and culture. These avenues have been created and are directed by Satan. The ways that people *react* to them and the fact that Satan seems to have left no stone unturned, is what guides this world.

We will cover the mundane and more pedestrian areas like rock music, movies, and horror in general, which has served to *desensitize* the public to its true malevolence. Beyond this, we will look seriously into the area of *Satanic worship*, what it is, what it means for the world along with whether it is actually happening or is merely a figment of people's overworked imaginations due to the proliferation of movies with horror and paranormal themes.

Is there a connection between rock music *and* Satanism? Undoubtedly, you may have heard that charge before and maybe you believe that *"it's just music. What harm can it do?"* Well, maybe it is time to revisit the subject to see if anything has changed over the years.

Rock by Any Other Name
Rock music has been around since before the 1950s. It has changed and grown into many genres. Because of that, it has become known

by a multitude of names and while these are not all the same type of music, the similarity between them should be noted. Essentially, all of these labels come together under one heading and this is only a very partial listing of all the labels that apply to music that comes under the heading of "Heavy Metal."

1. Acid Rock
2. Alternative Rock
3. Black Metal
4. Blackened Death Metal
5. Celtic Punk
6. Celtic Rock
7. Christian Metal
8. Classic Metal
9. Dark Metal
10. Death Core
11. Death Metal
12. Grunge Metal
13. Hard Rock
14. Heavy Metal
15. Horror Punk
16. Industrial Metal
17. Industrial Rock
18. Pagan Rock
19. Power Metal
20. Power Violence
21. Punk Rock
22. Screamo
23. Shock Rock
24. Sleaze Rock
25. Sludge Metal
26. Speed Metal
27. Speed Rock
28. Thrash Metal

The previous list is but a small cross section of the various names that are included in the rock genre. Notice that there is such a thing as "Christian Metal" (number 7). Is the Christian community taking its cue from the world? It would seem so, though that is nothing new.

All of the above listings have a number of things in common:

- *Excessively loud volume*
- *Often overly fast-paced*
- *Very heavy on drums and bass*
- *Mesmerizing and energizing*
- *Encourages release of inhibitions*
- *Very "tribal" at its root*
- *Either overt or hidden references to Satan and the occult*

In a three hour DVD produced by Pastor Joe Schimmel, president of Fight the Good Fight Ministries, we gain a great deal of insight into how the enemy has worked and continues to work. At the beginning of the DVD, we see the crowds before *Ozzfest*, a multiple-day concert event started by Ozzie Osborne, and the bands that perform there are of the same caliber as Black Sabbath, the band Ozzie used to front.

A reporter asks concertgoers whether they believe that the type of music played at Ozzfest is demonic or Satanic in any way. Of the ones they asked, all of them agreed that it was *not*. To them, it is just music, nothing more. This is in spite of the fact that many artists have literally sold their souls to Satan.

Bob Pittman, founder of MTV Network has stated, *"The strongest appeal you can make is emotionally. If you can get their emotions going, make them forget their logic, you've got 'em."*[35] He is also quoted as saying, *"At MTV, we don't shoot for the 14-year-olds, we own them."*[36]

---

[35] Fight the Good Fight DVD (Simi Valley), www.goodfight.org
[36] Ibid

The tragedy here is that Pittman is *correct*. There is something so powerful in music that people can connect with it almost instantly and they do so, on a purely emotional level. It not only sways their emotions, but it *guides* the way they think because their thinking stems from the emotional charge they receive from listening to the music they like. Rolling Stones' Keith Richards is quoted as saying, *"once it goes in, you have essentially no ability to say what it does to you."*[37] Music has the ability to change the emotional state of the mind *powerfully* and *immediately*.

If we take a close look at a few bands, we will certainly get the gist of what their message is all about and we will ascertain what, if any impact these bands have on society. Before we do that, it is important to note that since Satan has the keys to this world, so to speak, it seems that what he has done is created on large mindset of entertainment. In other words, the world has fast become a playground of sorts for evil. People want to have fun, they want to release any pent up stress, and they prefer to see life as an adventure.

Satan has provided numerous ways for people to get what they want and music is simply one of the ways to accomplish that, along with movies, which we will get into shortly. Once you get people hooked on specific genres, it is difficult for them to break its tenacious hold and they wind up succumbing to the attitudes and demeanor of the messages built into the songs along with the antics of the performers.

Years ago, in 1971, John Lennon produced a song called *"Imagine."* It had a great tune. I remember humming along to it and even singing the words at times. Once I actually noticed the lyrics, I finally came to the realization (I'm sure with God's help) that the song is not only anti-Christian and anti-God, but glorifies the atheistic belief-system and worldview. Here are some of the lyrics:

---

[37] Fight the Good Fight DVD (Simi Valley), www.goodfight.org

> *Imagine there's no heaven*
> *It's easy if you try*
> *No hell below us*
> *Above us only sky*
> *Imagine all the people*
> *Living for today...*
> *Imagine there's no countries*
> *It isn't hard to do*
> *Nothing to kill or die for*
> *And no religion too*
> *Imagine all the people*
> *Living life in peace...*

Certainly, some of what John wrote has a nice ring to it and who does not want all war to end? Who does not want true peace? Notice that aside from Lennon's thoughts about no God, he also is actually wishing for one world with no divisions at all. The idea is that all people, living together in complete peace, with no wars or revolutions, and no presidents, leaders or dictators is a complete pipedream, especially for fallen humanity. There will come a day when the entire world will be one, but it will be ruled and overseen by Jesus Christ Himself, during the Millennial Kingdom. Prior to that, Antichrist will have his chance to shine, and will be the last world ruler prior to Jesus dispatching Him with the breath of His mouth upon His return.

Regarding Lennon's song, and others like it, these songs stay with a person for years, and can and do become part of a person's cognition and worldview without even realizing it. Songs like this tend to set the stage for a spiritual revolution and overhaul in a person's life. I believe that is exactly what has happened over the past number of decades.

However, not everyone listens to mellow music like "Imagine" because not all are built that way. Many people seem to run on raw adrenalin and because of that, they adopt a musical style that suits them. Many rock bands fit the bill of providing adrenalin rushes, inducing a type of hyperactive lawlessness. It would take more than one book to catalog the bands and their connection – directly or indirectly – to Satanism and Satan. However, it might surprise people how even seemingly innocuous bands include members that lead lives devoted to Satan. There are simply too many bands and individual musical artists to note, so we will only take the time to look at just a few.

One thing to realize is that this author is *not* saying, implying, or charging that all bands noted here are deliberately Satanic in nature. In fact, it appears that even with those bands who are overtly Satanic in nature, by using symbolism, and lyrics, as well as costumes and props on stage, are so out of a sense of

Black Sabbath's "Born Again"

Grim Reaper's "See You in Hell"

Possessed's "Beyond the Gate"

entertainment value, giving people what they want. They do not necessarily do what they do because they themselves are Satanists. Evil, horror, and Satan *sells*. Like businesspeople who want to hook as many people as possible into buying their music, many bands today use numerous gimmicks in order to make that happen. It is clear though that too many bands believe to have actual connections with Satan himself.

Slayer's "Reign in Blood"

It may also be that the producers of the music, or the record labels themselves are run by people who are Satanists, or part of the Illuminati. There are too many bands and artists using occult symbolism for all of this to be a coincidence.

Judas Priest's "Sin After Sin"

However, while the bands themselves might not be deliberately choosing to pull from the arena of Satanism to enhance their music, the responsibility still lies with them for the message they are sending out to millions of people via their music and their presentation.

Testament's "The New Order"

Groups and individuals like *Tool, Shakira, Slipknot, Korn, Gwen Stefani, Marilyn Manson, Adam Lambert, Lady Gaga,* and others all use Freemason symbolism, the all-seeing eye. Other groups are overt as well, in either their name, their costuming, or their lyrics. Groups like Black Sabbath, fronted by Ozzy Osborne have written songs about Aleister Crowley for instance, noted occultist from the early 1900s. Among other things, Crowley called himself "Antichrist," and wrote instructions on how to sacrifice children to conjure up demons. Another group *Grim Reaper*, has a song called "See You Hell My Friend," "All Hell Let Loose," "Lord of Darkness" and others from their dual CD *See You in Hell/Fear No Evil*. The band Grim Reaper also produced other albums/CDs titled, *Rock You to Hell.*

Black Sabbath has produced albums/CDs titled *We Sold Our Soul for Rock n Roll, Heaven & Hell, Mob Rules, Dehumanizer, Live Evil, Sabbath, Bloody Sabbath* and others. When lead singer Ozzy Osborne left the group, Ronny James Dio took over lead singing responsibilities. While he toured with Sabbath, they used the name *Heaven & Hell* (instead of Black Sabbath). One of their first CDs together is called *The Devil You Know*. Mr. Dio recently died from cancer at 67.

Other bands like *Grave Digger, Anvil, Krokus, Helloween, Overkill, Iron Maiden, Judas Priest, Hellstar, Charred Walls of the Damned, Autopsy, Killer Dwarfs, Slayer, Demon, Possessed* and more all have imagery and lyrics that nod to Satan, demons, and the power of the dark lord.

Do the artists themselves want to use symbols and lyrics that glorify Satan? It would appear that the bands *and* the record labels are knowingly pushing these things on the youth of today. Soon, it will be so commonplace that no one will bat an eyelid at any of it. Parents who simply ignore what their kids are listening to are simply creating situations in which more and more kids will become walking time bombs, like Eric Harris and Dylan Klebold, known for their massacre of students at Columbine. *"News reports have indicated that Dillon Klebold and Eric Harris had been on a long road that was littered with depravity. Their obsessive and repetitive viewing of violent videos, engagement in murderous computer games and collecting of exotic weaponry should have alerted their parents that something was terribly wrong."*[38] These two senior high students and their foray into the subculture world of the gothic and macabre, along with the music they listened to – among them the band *Marilyn Manson* – and videos and movies they watched all created a troubled worldview and path for the two young men.

For society to continue to believe and claim that what people hear, see, and participate in, does not affect them is ludicrous. It seems clear enough from even recent history that Hollywood, TV, and music has together perpetrated a crime against humanity. They have succeeded in brainwashing millions for their own sadistic pleasure and satanic goals. It has become too obvious to ignore, yet it continues because while people are aware of it, because they see it mainly as *entertainment*, they see no real harm in it. Quite the contrary is true though, and it is this author's opinion that the situation will only become much worse as time marches on toward the final climax of world history.

Marilyn Manson

Brian Hugh Warner of Canton, Ohio came into the world on January 5, 1969. His father was Catholic, his mother was Episcopalian, and he attended a Christian school for most of his education. After graduating from high school, he studied at Broward Community College in journalism. He eventually walked away from religion altogether, forming a band called *Marilyn Manson and the Spooky Kids*. *"The band is one of modern music's most controversial, due largely to frequent clashes with religious and political figures. The name of each band member was originally created by combining the first name of an iconic female sex symbol (e.g. Marilyn Monroe), and the last name of an iconic mass murderer or serial killer (e.g. Charles Manson). The mem-*

---

[38] http://www.firstliberties.com/killing_fields_childhood.html

bers of the band dress in outlandish makeup and costumes, and have engaged in intentionally shocking behavior both onstage and off. Their lyrics often receive criticism for their anti-religious sentiment and their references to sex, violence, and drugs. Marilyn Manson's music and performances have frequently been called offensive and obscene, and, on several occasions, protests and petitions have led to the group being banned from performing."[39]

Manson is included on the Fight the Good Fight DVD previously mentioned, and in one clip from a live concert, Manson can be heard yelling, *"we will no longer be oppressed by the fascism of Christianity!"*[40] Manson's obscenity and hatred of Christianity is one of the ideologies that motivate him, and this hatred of Christianity, as can be seen, is passed onto his fans. He has become an evangelist for Satan and he is likely pleased about that.

DMX

There are too many rock bands and rap groups to list. Most rap groups are hardcore, leaving nothing to the imagination. In one of the DMX's songs, the lyrics are *"I'm comin' in the house, and I'm gunnin' for your spouse, tryin' to send the (expletive) back to her maker..."* and *"and if you got a daughter older than 15, I'm a rape her. Take her on the living room floor right there in front of you. I'm gonna make you suffer, see your (expletive) in hell"* (followed by gunshots).

One of the clips included on the Fight the Good Fight DVD showed DMX in concert singing/rapping this song. The crowd was *huge* and they were all clapping and rapping right along with DMX. The lyrics describe breaking into someone's house and killing a woman. Then, taking the daughter (if she is older than 15) and raping her right in front of her father! The gunshots following the lyrics obviously mean that death will come at the end. How is this anything *but* Satanic? It

---

[39] http://en.wikipedia.org/wiki/Marilyn_Manson_(band)
[40] Fight the Good Fight DVD (Simi Valley), www.goodfight.org

can be nothing else? Why would anyone sing or rap this and think it is *art*? How is it people listen to this and believe it to be worth listening to? It is incredible.

Rush
This band hails from Canada and goes back a long way. To their credit, they seem to have avoided the personnel

problems that plague most bands. There have only been two changes in personnel and that happened immediately after release of their very first album. The then current drummer John Rutsey, left the band in 1974 due to health problems and was replaced by Neil Peart. The other member to leave was bassist Jeff Jones, replaced by Geddy Lee only a few weeks after the band formed.

Aside from this, to this author's knowledge, the band has never been caught up in arrests, brawls, drugs, or any other things that bring notoriety to many rock groups. The three members of the group are hard working and do their best to recreate the songs live in concert as they were recorded in the studio.

That aside, through their lyrics, Rush often connects to the mystical and even paranormal. Besides drumming, Neil Peart mainly writes all lyrics. He has an eclectic interest in philosophy, as well as following Ayn Rand's atheistic "Objectivism."

Objectivism is defined as *"Objectivism holds that reality exists independent of consciousness; that individual persons are in direct contact with reality through sensory perception; that human beings can gain objective knowledge from perception through the process of concept formation and inductive and deductive logic; that the proper moral purpose of one's life is the pursuit of one's own happiness or rational self-interest; that the only social system consistent with this morality is full respect for individual rights, embodied in pure laissez faire capitalism; and that the role of art in human life is to transform man's widest metaphysical ideas, by selective reproduction of reality, into a physical form—a work of art—that he can comprehend and to which he can respond emotionally."*[41]

On Rush's album titled, "2112," at least one included song incorporated Rand's Objectivist leanings. The song starts with the Scripture verse *"And the meek shall inherit the earth,"* as the Overture, and then moves into the second part of the song subtitled, *"The Temples of Syrinx."* Some of lyrics are,

> *We've taken care of everything*
> *The words you hear, the songs you sing*
> *The pictures that give pleasure to your eyes.*
> *It's one for all and all for one*
> *We work together, common sons*
> *Never need to wonder how or why.*
> *We are the Priests of the Temples of Syrinx*
> *Our great computers fill the hallowed halls.*
> *We are the Priests, of the Temples of Syrinx*
> *All the gifts of life are held within our walls.*
> *Look around at this world we've made*
> *Equality our stock in trade*
> *Come and join the Brotherhood of Man*
> *Oh, what a nice, contented world*
> *Let the banners be unfurled*
> *Hold the Red Star proudly high in hand.*
> *We are the Priests of the Temples of Syrinx*

---

[41] http://en.wikipedia.org/wiki/Objectivism_(Ayn_Rand)

Our great computers fill the hallowed halls.
We are the Priests, of the Temples of Syrinx
All the gifts of life are held within our walls.[42]

There is certainly a humanistic, anti-God stance in that song, along with the use of the pentagram on the CD's cover. However, Rush's latest CD and its cover art are probably the most overt.

Clockwork Angels (shown above) has a clock featured on the cover and instead of using numerals to signify the time, Rush has chosen to use occult *symbolism*. Starting where the number 12 would be and moving clockwise, the symbols are: *brimstone, torrefaction of gold, mercury, winter, zinc, sun or gold, water or Aquarius, essence, Neptune, solve, earth or blackening, and copper.*

---

[42] Lyrics by Peart with acknowledgement to the genius of Ayn Rand

Why Rush decided to be so overt about it is not known at this point since the album is barely out in stores, but over the coming months, the public will certainly know much more about it.

Rolling Stones
In many ways, this next band has been around seemingly forever and has had numerous hits. A number of songs cater directly to Satan, such as *Sympathy for the Devil*. Here is a sampling of lyrics.

> *Please allow me to introduce myself*
> *I'm a man of wealth and taste*
> *I've been around for a long, long year*
> *Stole many a man's soul and faith*
> *And I was 'round when Jesus Christ*
> *Had his moment of doubt and pain*
> *Made damn sure that Pilate*
> *Washed his hands and sealed his fate*
> *Pleased to meet you*
> *Hope you guess my name*
> *But what's puzzling you*
> *Is the nature of my game*

Another album they produced (their sixth), is titled, *Their Satanic Majesties Request.* It is clear from not only the title, but also the lyrics and the album art themselves that this group of individuals reveres Aleister Crowley. The Satanic references and implications to him are everywhere on this CD.

Aleister Crowley is the patron saint of rock and roll and referred to himself as the beast and 666. In a very real sense, Crowley is the father of modern Satanism. Though raised in a Christian home, he forsook his Christian upbringing knowingly, deliberately choosing Satan over God. He did not *doubt* the teachings of Christianity, but simply rejected them outright in favor of the teachings of the Dark Lord.

The Beatles
The Beatles are probably the quintessential band that was a major turning point in music. Originally, their music seemed mundane and innocent, though young people could not get enough of them. Songs like, *I Want to Hold Your Hand, A Hard Day's Night, Help!,* and a multitude of other hits, catapulted the band to international stardom, seemingly overnight.

It was not long though, before the quirky and even dark side of the Beatles came to the fore. *Sgt. Pepper's Lonely Hearts Club Band* was a psychedelic rock album, which astounded critics due to the complexity of the music itself. It also contained references to the occult on the album's cover. Individuals like *Sri Yukteswar Giri (Hindu guru), Aleister Crowley (occultist), Carl Gustav Jung (psychologist), Aldous Huxley (writer), Sri Mahavatar Babaji (Hindu guru), Karl Marx (political philosopher), Sri Paramahansa Yogananda (Hindu guru) Sigmund Freud (psychiatrist), Sri Lahiri Mahasaya (guru), Lewis Carroll (writer)*, and other more innocuous people graced the cover of the album. It was not long after this that the Beatles began somewhat of an association with Maharishi Mahesh Yogi and his system of Transcendental Meditation. Many within the United States quickly picked this up and TM (as it became known), soon became a staple in our culture.

There is a tremendous amount of satanic references on the Sgt. Pepper album art. People, symbols, and even a representation of the woman from the book of Revelation can be seen.

The lyrics "*It was 20 years ago today Sgt Pepper taught the band to play*", is believed to be a reference to Crowley. The album was released 20 years after (almost to the day), Crowley died.

Backward Masking

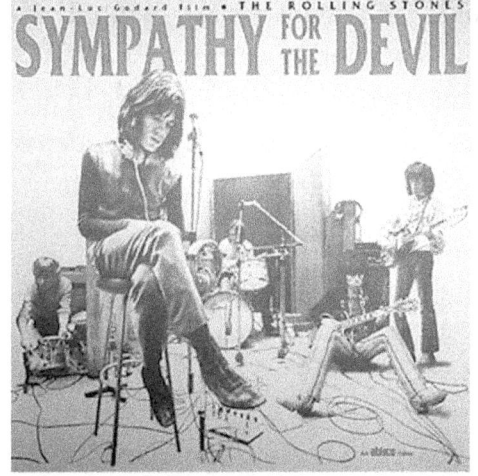

Backward masking is the concept of either deliberately or not, placing words or phrases on songs when played *backwards*. Does it exist? If so, how does it get there?

There are any number of theories regarding this phenomenon. One wonders why this would even be necessary anymore with the way some lyrics without apology expose the true meaning of the artist's thoughts and beliefs. We will take a look at a number of them (besides the ones we have already looked at), to get an overall picture of what is being sung to the youth of today.

It certainly appears as if it is in fact a reality. There are too many incidents of backward masking to be coincidental. There is really only one possible reason for it to be included on CDs, and that is *mind control*. In a chapter later on in this book, we will investigate this subject, but for now, let's go under the belief that backward masking *is real*, and that it is there for a *purpose.* As noted, the purpose would have to be related to mind control, getting the populace to believe something other than what they might normally believe. It is not good to have individuals that do not *go with the flow*, or appear to stand in opposition to the idea of a totalitarian regime that would hold sway over the entire world.

If people are going to submit to a coming one-world order, the first thing that must be done is to break down their defenses, and tear away the absolutes that they may have grown up with, absolutes that are opposed to a one-world regime.

To do this, society needs to have a system in place (hidden from view and "heard" only subconsciously), that overrides a person's current worldview and belief system. This system needs to operate 24 hours a day, 365 days per year to overrule a person's internal make up so that they become susceptible to a *new* frame of mind.

A system like this, needs to be part of *all* aspects of society. It needs to be resident within TV shows, movies, and music. It needs to be embedded in advertising, politically correct speech and other areas that will override a person's worldview by bombarding people on a daily basis, moment, by moment.

There are many videos on the Internet in which people have simply recorded popular songs *backwards.* The listener can decide for him or herself if what they hear are actual words, and if words, what those words say. One individual placed up a video of the Led Zeppelin song, "Stairway to Heaven," that most of us are familiar with from our youth. Interestingly enough, many of these songs are making strong comebacks today for a new generation of young people.

The words of the song are, in part:

> *"If there's a bustle in your hedgerow*
> *Don't be alarmed now*

> *It's just a spring clean for the may queen*
> *Yes, there are two paths you can go buy*
> *But in the long run*
> *There's still time to change the road you're on."*[43]

The same person who created the video indicates that the following is heard when playing this part of the song *backwards*:

> *So here's to my sweet Satan*
> *There's one whose little path*
> *Would make me sad,*
> *Whose power is Satan.*
> *He'll give you 666*
> *There was a little tool shed*
> *Where he made us suffer. Sad Satan.*

Are those words really there? I listened to it and some of the verbiage is very clear, while some of it is not. Is it coincidence? It could be, but as we start investigating more of these types of songs, we have to ask ourselves about the possibility of all of this simply being coincidental.

It is a known fact that subliminal messages often affect the way people think, their likes and dislikes. We also know that experiments on advertising have been done in the past that prove the susceptibility of people to these subconscious suggestions. In that case, would there be a reason for subliminal messages on a recorded song?

Crowley said *"Let him learn to write backwards, with either hand, Let him learn to walk backwards, Let him constantly watch, if convenient, cinematograph films, and listen to the phonograph records, reversed, and let him so accustom himself to these that they appear natural and*

---
[43] Song composed by Jimmy Page and Robert Plant. ©1971. All rights reserved.

appreciable as a whole."[44] This would also explain why Anton LaVey and other Satanists say the Lord's Prayer *backwards*.

More interestingly though is that it is hardly likely that in the case of "Stairway to Heaven," the producers or singer actually took the time to *create* a message that when played backwards says something else entirely. If that is so, then what we have to consider is that there can only be three possibilities:

1. *Backward masking in which audibly understood phrases are included is a complete coincidence*
2. *People are simply believing that they hear something when they are really hearing nothing out of the ordinary*
3. *Satan is working through the artists to write songs in such a way that create specific verbiage when played backwards*

Let's say that it truly is *number 3*, and Satan has worked through these artists (many of whom seem sold out to him anyway), to get phrases that he wants onto these recordings. If so, then we must ask whether these backwardly masked recordings have the ability to actually *stick with* and *make a difference* in a person's mindset.

Another person takes the same section of the same song by Zeppelin and reverses it. The words *they* discover from the reversed playback is nearly identical, with some minor differences.

Oh here's to my sweet Satan
The one whose little path would make me sad
Whose power is Satan
He'll give those with him 666
There was a little tool shed
Where he made us suffer. Sad Satan.

---

[44] Fight the Good Fight DVD (Simi Valley), www.goodfight.org

With respect to *Stairway*, there are numerous satanic references throughout the song *and* the artwork. First, Robert Plant admitted that the lyrics to the song were given to him via *automatic writing*.

This seems to be the case with many rock and roll artists. One after the other claims that words, full songs, and even concert sets have come to them "out of the blue" with no effort on their part. They almost feel bad taking credit for the songs, because they do not feel they wrote them so much as they simply wrote them *down*.

Schimmel (from Fight the Good Fight) points out that the "stairway" in the song leads to *outer darkness* and the hermit (from the artwork) represents the occult (based on Aleister Crowley's hermit drawn by Crowley himself). The term "May Queen" is from a poem written by Aleister Crowley.

The lyrics, *"There are two paths you can go by – the piper is calling you to join me"* references the path to heaven or the path to hell. Satan has pipes associated with him as does Pan. The phrase *"Whispering Wind"* is often associated with Satan's path.

The interesting thing that stands out from many in the rock arena is their own belief that they are *possessed* in some form or another. Glenn Benton of the band *Deicide* says that his music is a focal point to express his Satanism to his fan base. Benton not only believes in demonic possession but also without equivocation says he *IS* possessed. He also stated, *"I believe in torment. I believe in a lot of pain in the end of my existence."*[45] One of the songs from Benton's band says, *"In hell I burn, no questions remain. In hell I burn for Satan."*

Benton did not stop there though. He pointed out *"I collect souls. That's what I do. If I can collect one soul…if I can convert one person to accepting evil as part of their lives…"*[46] This is how the hounds of hell

---

[45] Fight the Good Fight DVD (Simi Valley), www.goodfight.org
[46] Ibid

will take over the world, by infesting and *possessing* millions of people on the earth!

It is important for authentic Christians to realize that this is how hard Satan is working through his "musical" evangelists on the earth with every concert, every song, every CD, every lyric. How much *more* should Christians be out there evangelizing?

These lyrics are obvious. They hold nothing back. They say it as it is believed. However, the writers, the musicians, and the fans that listen and agree are all *deceived*. That is the tragedy.

As far as backward masking is concerned, the same individual referred to earlier, also took the Queen song, "Another One Bites the Dust" and reversed it. The repeated phrase by front man Freddie Mercury, *"another one bites the dust"* became *"it's fun to smoke marijuana."*

Stephen L. Gibson of *Truth Driven*, does a reverse on Michael J. Smith's song, "I'm Gone." Gibson does not believe that there is anything to backward masking. He explains the phenomenon as being similar to looking up into the sky and seeing clouds. As kids, we would try to see if there were any patterns to the clouds, and sometimes, we would see "images" in the clouds. This is our brain attempting to put patterns together to create something understandable to us. Gibson believes this is exactly what happens with the backward masking.

When playing Smith's song backwards, Gibson plays it without saying, what he *thinks* might be heard. Then he tells us *what* to listen for and plays it again.

Gibson may have a point. I listened to some of the videos without watching them so that I would not see any words put up by the individual who created the video. In many cases, I could not discern actual words, while in other cases I *could* hear words that sounded like "devil," or "Satan," or "dead" or phrases like "I was here." This does not prove anything. Who knows the truth about this subject? Certainly, everyone has an opinion, but opinions do not make facts.

Frankly, I would not put it past Satan to work through various rock artists who have likely sold their souls to him for success, to give them words to songs that when played backwards *can be understood* to say something about him (Satan). That is not beyond the realm of possibility.

However, as noted, do we really need to go there? Many bands do not even try to hide a subliminal message in their lyrics, forget about backward masking. They say it like it is and they seem proud of it too. Society has gotten to the point where the dam seems to have burst and the gates have opened to allow much of what artists want to say through their songs, to be said. Just slap a "WARNING" sticker on the cover of the CD and voilá! problem solved. Let's take a look at a few more.

Black Sabbath
Here are lyrics by the group *Black Sabbath*, called "Black Sabbath."

"Black Sabbath"

What is this that stands before me?
Figure in black which points at me
Turn around quick, and start to run
Find out I'm the chosen one
Oh no
Big black shape with eyes of fire
Telling people their desire
Satan's sitting there, he's smiling
Watches those flames get higher and higher

Satanic Strategies

Oh no, no, please God help me
Is it the end, my friend?
Satan's coming 'round the bend
People running 'cause they're scared
The people better go and beware
No, no, please, no

It looks like the song is about death, with Satan on his way to take people. While the author of the song is calling out to God, it may be too little, too late.

Alice in Chains

This one asks questions that wind up mocking God and misrepresenting His character.

"God Am"
(sure gods all powerful.
But, does he have lips? whoa...)
Dear god, how have you been, then?
I'm not fine, f**k pretending
All of this death you're sending
Best throw some free heart mending
Invite you in my heart, then
When done, my sins forgiven?
This god of mine relapses
World dies I still pay taxes
Can I be as my god am
Can you be as god am
Can I be as my god am
God of all my god am

So lord, I see you grinnin'
Must be grand always winning
How proud are you being able
To gather faith from fable

Avenge Sevenfold

Allegedly, the members of this band have a Roman Catholic upbringing, which explains why many of their songs have religious connotations. This is a short tune (lyrically) that speaks of the Rapture, but seems to end in hopelessness.

"To End the Rapture"

The wind of life and air from above smells of death.
Angels sing of the end.
Nothing you say and nothing you try can change time.
Human race prepares to die...

Here's another one of Avenge Sevenfold's songs, this one about Babylon, the Fallen, likely based on Revelation 14. Below are part of the lyrics of the song.

"Beast and the Harlot"

This shining city built of gold, a far cry from innocence,
There's more than meets the eye round here, look to the waters of the deep.
A city of evil.
There sat a seven-headed beast, ten horns raised from his head.
Symbolic woman sits on his throne, but hatred strips her and leaves her naked.
The Beast and the Harlot.

She's a dwelling place for demons.
She's a cage for every unclean spirit,
every filthy bird and makes us drink
the poisoned wine to fornicating with our kings.
Fallen now is Babylon the Great.

Faith No More
This band is crude, to say the least, and they seem to be fixated on sexual situations and death. Some of the lyrics below are omitted so as not to offend.

"Highway I-35"

Wrath
Purifying the scum of the earth
I was born to murder the world
I'm a tool created by your apathic society
Feeding on my sadistic intent
Bleed bleed bleed for the (expletive) god
I murdered over thirty and still crave more
Kneel kneel kneel for the (expletive) god
I batter your genitals to pulp
Sculpture of my tormented thoughts
Crushing gutting tearing your limbs apart
As chunks of demormed meat
Are dripping from my knife
Consumed by frustration
Murder is my salvation
Coagulated (expletive), bursting

Satanic Strategies

> *Through the stomach wall*
> *I suck your (expletive) bloodtide*
> *Died by my hand*
> *I shall dismember and sever*
> *Died by my hand*

Fields of Nephilim
This band is dark as might be imagined. The lyrics below are from their CD, "Burning in the Fields"

> *"Back In Gehenna"*

> *All Great plains of the Earth*
> *Are now lighted by fire*
> *Now gather under wrecked land*
> *From these horsemen in iron*
> *This is the fear*
> *And all you've turned up*
> *Now the atmosphere*
> *Is thicker than blood*
> *From Gehenna to here*
> *A release of sin*
> *It's become our lair*
> *We!*
> *The Nephilim*
> *See the woman thrive*
> *In the blood from Heaven*
> *Burn in banished fire*
> *Like a scene called Hell*

See the bloody fire
To you is forsaken
Burn this bloody fire
Burn
Burn Hell

Godsmack
The lyrics below are from their Faceless CD.

"Release the Demons"

What do you see in the dark
When the demons come for you
If only you could have seen
How f**ked up my life used to be
Then everything starts to change
Supposedly healing my pain
I never thought I'd feel this way
I never thought that I'd see a day
I'd run away from anything or anywhere or anyone
It's all these demons haunting me
It's all these little things trapped inside of me
Releasing me from all my sin
It's taken me all my anger
And taken me all of my hate
To learn how my life came together
Releasing the demons again

Judas Priest
Judas Priest is a heavy metal band that often uses anti-religious lyrics

to make their point. The lyrics here are the first verse of the song, "Saints in Hell."

> They laughed at their gods
> And fought them in vain
> So he turned his back on them
> And left them in pain
> Now here come the saints
> With their banners held high
> Each one of them martyrs
> Quite willing to die

The lyrics from a multitude of other bands' music could be listed, each highlighting a particular piece that they bring to the overall puzzle. If you can imagine these songs with powerful electric guitar chords, heavy drumbeats, with a driving bass line, and plenty of volume, you can begin to understand what drives the youth of today.

Many of the lead singers of the aforementioned bands have vocalists that literally scream out the words, with very high-pitched, melodic, yet edgy singing.

"Nocturne" from PlayStation 2

"Devil Summoner" from PlayStation 2

Whether bands use Satanism as a selling point or not, is unclear. Nevertheless, it is obvious that Satan *is* a selling point. The idea seems to be to take that, which has always been viewed as verboten, and put it out there in the mainstream. This makes it (Satanism) approachable, nothing to be really feared.

An interest in Satan grew from humble beginnings until it became what it is now. Originally enamored with this new topic, over time, people have become so used to the symbolism, the imagery, the lyrics, and the music connected to it, that it is now taken for granted. It has become deeply engrained and fully accepted within the psyche of young people everywhere and ultimately, in society throughout the world. Because Satan has worked so diligently, consistently, and secretly to recreate the way human beings view him and the worship of him, this new less fearsome understanding of Satan has become permanently melded into the fabric of our thinking like nothing else.

"Shadow Hearts" by Playstation 2

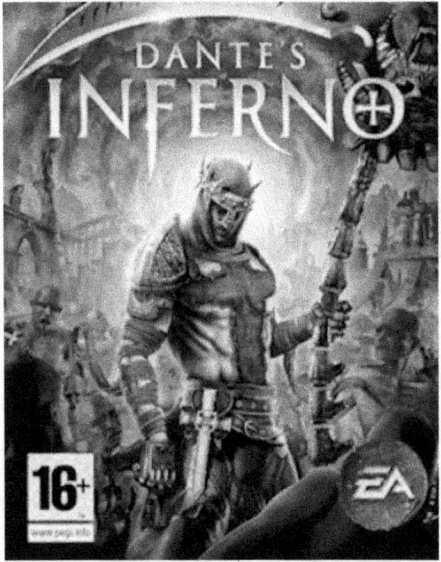

"Dante's Inferno" by EA

Video Games

However, it is not just music and lyrics that have reworked society. Video games, movies, and TV have also worked their spells to cause a huge shift in thinking. When video games began, they were innocent. Most remember Pong, or Pac Man, but before long, other games came along. Graphics got far better and racing games were introduced.

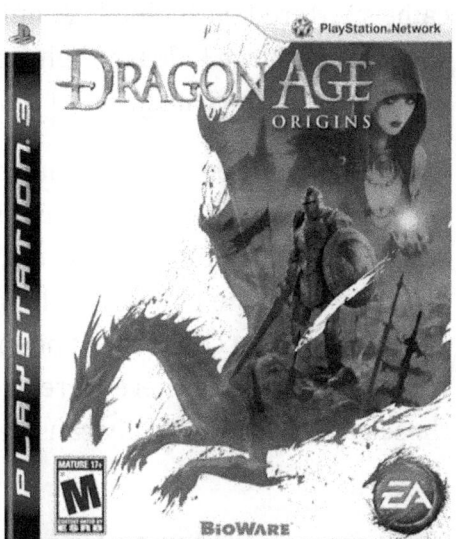

It was not long before RPG (role-playing games), or first person shooters came on the scene. From hunting monsters and ugly creatures, games put the player in the position of hunting other *humans*. While these may have started out as obvious fictional games (like Dracula, etc.), or war games, they soon turned into games where one person would hunt and kill other humans on the opposing teams.

As graphics became better and better, more blood and guts were added to the mix. At first, there was an option to turn "off" the blood and gore after someone was shot. After awhile, that option was gone and everything be-

came spattered with blood. People were not just shot. They were shot leaving large holes in their bodies, while their internal organs cascaded out onto the ground!

People soon got bored with your basic car racing game, so other options had to be added to the games to keep interest. *Grand Theft Auto* started out as a type of race game, but the idea was to steal a car and get away from the police. Not long afterwards, it morphed into a game where you could shoot people before you carjacked them, or rough them up, and there were even sexual situations included in these games. This initially caused some protests, but they quickly died.

Video games have come a long way from those text-based games where you merely read the text on the black monitor screen. I recall playing the game "Mist" years ago. All you saw was text describing the situation and giving you options.

"You are at the end of a large hall. There is a door on your left and one on your right." You would think about your options and then type in *"L"* or *"R"* to tell the computer what door you wanted to go in. After that, the computer would respond with something like, *"The door opens and you walk into a room with a door on the far wall to your left. There is a box on the floor in front of you. It is locked."*

This was the type of game we played, and believe it or not, it was scary because at any moment, something might jump out from somewhere and you would be told, *"A creature has just jumped out of the closet and killed you!"* Then you start the game all over again. Our imaginations filled in the blanks with games like that.

It takes no imagination to play the video games they have today. All the imagination is built into the graphics of the game. All the player needs to do is become an expert with the controller and chances of winning are great.

The cover art for the games listed all have aspects that are Satanic. The following quoted information is from Free Republic website.[47] Nocturne is *"a game in which the hero (a demon) destroys the three archangels St. Michael, Gabriel and Raphael, then goes on to destroy God."*

The game Devil Summoner, *"Involves communicating with and recruiting demons. One demon tells the player 'That Catholic Church is such an eyesore' and in the end of the game, blows up the Church."*

Shadow Hearts is a video game in which *"the hero uses his power to intercept and destroy God and 'save the world.' Some games in this series are rated 'T'."* "T" stands for Teen.

Dante's Inferno is a game *"loosely based on the Divine Comedy, [the] player travels through nine circles of Hell, fighting demons, 'unbaptized babies' and other tormented souls. (This game is being considered for a movie by Universal Pictures.)"*

Dragon Age Origins is a *"game [that] revolves around the story of God going mad and cursing the world. A witch attacks believers and players can 'have sex' with her in a pagan act called 'blood magic' so she can 'give birth to a god.' Another scenario allows players to have sex with a demon in exchange for a boy's soul."*

Tecmo's Deception is where *"players 'make an unholy pact and sell their soul to Satan in exchange for power' with the object of the game being to ensure the resurrection of Satan and obtain his power. (This game is rated 'T' for teen.)"*

In Assasin's Creed, the *"main character is a Muslim assassin assigned to kill Christians."*

---

[47] http://www.freerepublic.com/focus/f-religion/2445647/posts

Now parents, do you think that it is your responsibility to determine what games are allowed in your home? If you think your kids are just playing "games," you need to think again. These games are changing the worldviews of kids all over the globe. The message built into these games is being transferred to your children and that only means *trouble*.

Again, we need to understand that Satan has infected every area of society with his perversion. What many label *Satanism*, in which people worship him and often include ritual killings of animals and even human beings, is merely one aspect of it.

In truth though, as we have stated, everything that is anti-God in society is a form of Satanism, because he has created it so that he will be *worshiped*. That is his goal, his desire, and the prime reason he does anything.

We can get a rough idea of this by viewing the two graphs (at the end of the book). In the first one (**Satanic Pyramid Leading**

Two movies from George Romero, "Day of the Dead" and "Dawn of the Dead"

Satanic Strategies

to One God), we can see how Satan has worked through the main areas of society – *Education, Business, Religion, Entertainment, and Politics* – to bring all things to *his* preconceived conclusion. It should be obvious that unless he transforms each of these areas, he cannot win. Of course, we know he will not win anyway, but as stated, he *must* work as if he will.

For this reason, every major area of society is impacted. He has worked over the years to transform the way education thinks and therefore teaches students. The goal of course is to overturn and replace God's morality for Satan's. Satan seeks to imbue society with humanism that is nothing more than man-centered *religion*. This line of thinking elevates humanity to a place we are not meant to be.

Movies

We have touched on this subject in previous books, but since they are part of the entertainment industry, it is especially helpful to go a bit deeper in order to grasp the full reality of how Satan has

turned the movie industry into his own calling card. Years ago, Universal released movies that are now referred to as *Classic Horror* movies. As scary as they *were*, they were tame by today's standards. In fact, most would consider them extremely boring if compared to the slash 'em up movies that roll out of Hollywood these days.

A number of things have happened that changed the industry drastically, since the big studios and what was known as the "studio system." Many years ago, when studio executives had a firm grasp on not only the movies that were made, but also their stable of stars they had under contract, movies were carefully chosen and depicted in a way that mirrored society then.

Gone with the Wind, *Robin Hood*, and a ton of other classics came to life on the silver screen and people were truly entertained. Those days slowly went away as society changed. Wars, nations, and financial upheavals around the globe caused studios to look again at the type of movies they made. Television had not yet been invented, so that was no threat. Something more was needed.

What society demanded, it got. This is the nature of human beings. We want something desperately, but eventually become bored with it and demand something else. Hollywood provided for us movies like *Rebel Without a Cause*, or *On the Waterfront*, or *A Streetcar Named Desire*, were all made for theatrical release.

What most of the public did not know then, was that many of these celebrities were homosexual, completely addicted to alcohol, drugs, or both, or had other serious problems, emotionally or psychologically. Often the studios wound up creating stars whose personal lives were a mess. They were addicted to drugs because they would take drugs to be awake, and then take drugs to go to sleep. Since the studio kept a close connection with the media, they were able to dictate what went into print. Had the Internet been alive then, this would not have been possible. Today, anyone with a cell phone can capture "news" and put it up on the 'Net before anyone has a chance to complain.

As time progressed, the horror movie went from classic, to *freakish*. George Romero's movies are considered classics today because of their *age*, the way they introduced a new type of horror movie into the mainstream, and because *they* are tame by today's standards.

Dawn of the Dead was a movie about the overcrowded conditions of hell apparently. Because of that, the dead had no choice but to walk among the living. Oh, and they had to eat and or kill the living too!

It was not long before horror movies began to come into their own with a new style and twist that had not been used before. In previous movies like *Dracula,* starring Bela Lugosi, the blood was hardly seen and much of the violence was implied.

Satanic Strategies

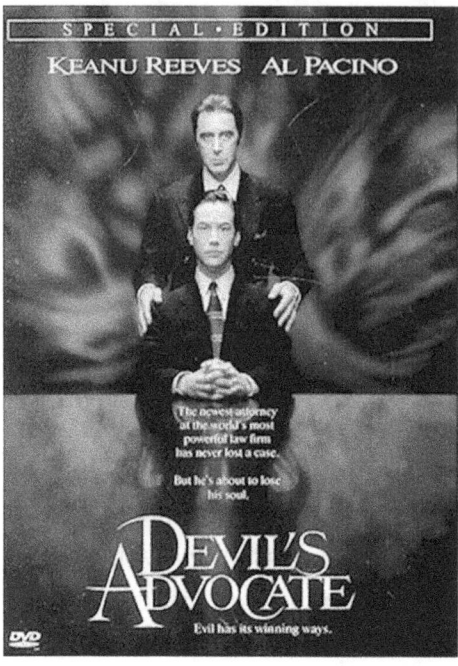

In the newer genre of movies by Romero and others, much less was left to the imagination. Horror was shown to be horrible, replete with blood, guts, dismembered arms, legs, and more! It is what the people wanted, so why not shock them? From here, the door opened and nothing was left to the imagination. There were still some schlocky horror movies like *Motel Hell* in which guests became part of the "garden" (planted in the dirt from the necks down). They had their vocal cords removed so they could not make much noise, and when the time was right, those poor folks became part of the pies that the woman who owned the hotel along with her husband, made. The sign in the movie says "Motel Hello" but the "o" is out.

It was not too much longer before the public was scared to death with the movie, *The Exorcist*, which is said to have been based on a true story. The screenplay was riveting, the effects were top notch, and the music was haunting.

I saw the movie against my parents' better judgment, and even though I laughed through some of it, I had nightmares that continued with me for quite some time. Other paranormal horror movies came to the screen, like *Rosemary's Baby*, *The Omen*, and many more. These movies always had the satanic theme running through them.

In *The Exorcist*, Satan came across as more powerful than at least one of the priests who attempted to exorcize Regan, the girl in the movie, played by Linda Blair.

Other movies seemed not to be able to get to the theaters fast enough! Many combined horror, with aliens, and sex. Hitting on all three areas would usually guarantee a hit.

Species came out, that was about an alien from outer space who came to the earth, picked up men, went home with them, and then mated with them. A number of follow up movies came after this one.

Another series of movies was the *Alien* franchise, starring Sigourney Weaver. In this case, people from earth went into space to find out what happened to others who had gone ahead of them. Earth had somehow lost contact with the first batch of astronauts. Upon arriving at the ship that held the first group, they discovered a very unwelcome sight, that of a monster that was very tall, had acid for blood and killed by ejecting a powerful inner jaw from her mouth. This split the skull of the victim nicely with blood everywhere.

However, the buying public gets tired of these types of movies because they obviously tend to come across as fake. What the public wanted was something that appeared to be so real, it would be difficult to deny. Hollywood obliged.

Movies soon became more realistic in dealing with the paranormal, aliens, and Satan. In *Devil's Advocate*, starring Al Pacino, Pacino plays either the Devil or one of his higher underlings. The movie contains

Satanic Strategies

graphic portrayals of demonic possession, and other supernatural and paranormal phenomenon.

Who can forget the franchises of *Halloween*, *Friday, the 13th*, and *Nightmare on Elm Street*? These movies bring in millions and beyond the movies, there are enough action figures, toys, and collectibles connected to each movie to make the creators of these films millionaires ten times over!

Of course, who can forget *Star Wars*, from LucasFilms? This movie, presented as science fiction, turned out to be something straight out

"Star Wars," from George Lucas, not only gave rise to any number of copycats and incarnations, but it serves as an instructional manual for the New Age.

The "Force" from the movie is basically the impersonal energy that can be tapped into by anyone. It has a dark side as well as a light side.

Darth Vader, the movie's villain was once on the side of light, but switched over to the dark side.

Luke, his son, remains firmly with the side of light, using the Force to overcome the obstacles placed in his path from those on the dark side.

Satanic Strategies

of the New Age Movement, replete with an impersonal "Force" that has two sides; dark and light.

The success of the movie prompted other sequels, prequels, and even cartoons based on the concept.

This new age of movies deals with paranormal, demonic, supernatural, and the occult and they do so without embarrassment because it is what the public wants. Folks, we have gone way past the point of no return. The only thing that can be done now is to evangelize as many people as possible so that God may open the eyes of those who receive salvation from Him.

Other movies that dealt with the Satanic or Illuminati are numerous. *The Matrix*, spawned three films in that genre, in which the main character discovered he was *in* a computerized matrix. In essence, computers and machines were using him and millions of other human be-

Satanic Strategies

ings. They harvested their energy while they were in a suspended animation state. The life they "lived" was actually all a *dream*. Waking up from the matrix was *reality*.

National Treasure starred Nicolas Cage and went to two movies. The movies are heavily laden with references to the Illuminati. Even one of the original *Batman* movies (starring Michael Keaton as Batman and Bruce Wayne) referenced the Illuminati. In the movie, *Batman Returns*, "*Max Shreck (Walken), is dressed as a genie with an all seeing eye inside of a pyramid placed on his head. At another point in the film he is shown displaying a model of a power plant he would like to build which is in the shape of a pyramid with the capstone missing.*"[48]

Wag the Dog was another film that purported to show a fictional account of how our government works behind the scenes, especially during elec-

---

[48] Mark Dice *The Illuminati Facts & Fiction* (The Resistance 2009), 363

tion times. In this movie, a Hollywood producer was brought in to create scenarios that would put the current president in a favorable light as election approached.

Television

Movies were great because during the Depression, it offered a chance to get away from the harsh realities of life, even if for only a few hours. Eventually Television broke onto the scene and as opposed to movies, began portraying everyday life as a *continual* situation. The early shows presented a father who was generally strong, wise, and the obvious head of the home. Mothers supported the husband and the kids understood their role as well.

Shows like *My Three Sons* and *Father Knows Best* highlighted good, wholesome, family-oriented viewing (even if a bit unrealistic). Over time, these shows gave way to another type of show, where the husband/father was increasingly taking a back seat to the mother. After this introduction was complete, the next step was to portray the father as a buffoon, or an outright idiot, with a wife

who always knows better and has the final say.

Father Knows Best and *My Three Sons* eventually gave way to shows like *Everybody Loves Raymond* and *Home Improvement*. In *Everybody Loves Raymond*, Ray Romano's character Ray, is a complete buffoon. His wife constantly outsmarts him and she is the one who always laying down the law. Ray is often intimidated by his wife and routinely becomes the butt of many jokes.

In *Home Improvement*, the father/husband character of Tim Taylor, played by Tim Allen, does not fair much better.

Wife Jill is constantly governing and herding the family and attempting to pick up the pieces from Tim's numerous failed projects. While he has good intentions, the inside joke is that Tim cannot really complete any household project without encountering problems.

Probably one of the worst shows that came onto the screen in the form of a sitcom in recent years was *Married with Children*, which was obnoxious; there was no value in watching it at all. Of course, the creators, writers, and actors will say that what they did was create an over the top caricature of married life. In truth, what they actually created was a sitcom in which the sanctity of marriage was denigrated every week.

In "Married," the wife hated the husband and vice versa, and the kids hated the parents and each other. All four were always trying to make deals with each other, or trying to schmooze mom or dad out of money for this or that. It wasn't much better where the wife and husband were concerned either, with constant barbs tossed at one another as put downs.

The Bill Cosby Show attempted to bring balance to the family, yet even here, the wife in the show, portrayed by Phylicia Rashad, was often presented as stronger than Cosby's character. Cosby had to kowtow often.

It was clear that Television appeared to be doing its best to *reshape* American culture. Gone forever were the days of *Father Knows Best* and *My Three Sons*, and in their place were shows in which roles were often defined by going outside the normative traits that for so long had been shown on TV.

The television show *24's*, main character Jack Bauer (portrayed by actor, Keifer Sutherland), continually sets the U.S. Constitution aside as the need arises. The underlying message is that the government can do whatever it wants to do in its pursuits and this of course, is reminiscent of how the Illuminati and the world's elite works. They consider themselves to be above the law because they are the law.

Charmed is another show about the supernatural. It involves three young women who are witches. *Pretty Little Lies* is hyped as a "family show" from ABC, and as this book was being written, had just begun airing. The show is heavy on the supernatural.

Satanic Strategies

"Lucy, the Daughter of the Devil," is a show about Satan attempting to convince his daughter that she needs to fulfill her role regarding the Antichrist. Jesus is depicted as a techno DJ and the Bohemian Grove is also a backdrop for the show, which airs on Adult Swim and is produced by the Cartoon Network. The show ran from October 2005 to November 2007 for a total of 11 episodes.

Adult Swim has had its share of bizarre characters, some directly connected to Satan, like *Lucy, Daughter of the Devil*. "*It is a ten minute CGI comedy with a plot involving Satan who lives in San Francisco and is trying to convince his 21-year-old daughter, Lucy, to fulfill her role as the Antichrist. Lucy's boyfriend is JD Jesus, a techno DJ who is actually Jesus Christ.*"[49] Apparently, the cartoon includes a depiction of the *Bohemian Grove* where the members of the Skull & Bones Society (a branch of the Illuminati) meet each year

Live-action TV shows are not the only things that have attempted to change America's outlook. Animated shows have changed in a major way. One of the earliest to buck the norm was a show called *Beavis & Butthead*.

---

[49] Mark Dice *The Illuminati Facts & Fiction* (The Resistance 2009), 375

These two high schoolers would be every teacher's nightmare and often were just that on the show. Teachers were left to throw up their hands in defeat.

Created by Mike Judge, the show was built around the inept and anti-social behavior of the two main characters. It was not long before every kid in America was imitating the speech and jokes of these two only to the delight of other teenagers.

King of the Hill was another animated sitcom created by Mike Judge. In this show, main character Hank Hill tries to keep his head and perspective all the while surrounded by idiots and neighborly nincompoops.

There were many events, which caused major frustration for Hank, but there were times of contentment and peace toward neighbors. The show made fun of those who were staunchly pro-American in the form of neighbor Dale Gribble, who was also a conspiracy theory buff. Another neighbor, Bill Dauterive, a less than intelligent (though

well meaning) lifelong friend of Hank lived down the block.

There was also the token Native American, who slept with Dale Gribble's wife on a regular basis. She became pregnant and gave birth to a son that looked very much like his Native American father, though Dale never noticed anything.

After its tenth season, this show was ultimately cancelled in order to put another animated show on the air. *Family Guy*, was a show that started out funny though the family itself was somewhat disjointed and quirky. Plain funny gets old and boring quickly, so it was not long before creator Seth McFarlane instilled the show with off-color jokes and sexual innuendo. It was only a very short time before the show became unwatchable.

The same thing happened in yet another animated sitcom, *American Dad*, also created by McFarlane. In fact, it was announced only a few days ago as this is being written, that *American Dad* was under investigation by the

FCC over a horse ejaculation scene. *"The Federal Communications Commission is proposing to fine Fox $25,000 for failing to properly respond to its questions about the airing of a Jan. 3 episode of 'American Dad' installment that drew 100,000 consumer complaints."*[50]

Of course, one good thing is that people are still willing to complain about things like this. The actual scene in the show was only *implied* and was eventually shown to be *water* that had been sprayed from a garden hose. Yet, the dialogue leading up to it was filled with sexual innuendo. This is the problem with many shows. They are unable to carry the humor they start out with over the long haul, so it changes.

They have to keep pushing the envelope more and more to satisfy the constantly changing whims of society in order to maintain precious *ratings*.

Cartoons Reach a New Low

We cannot forget two other shows

---

[50] http://www.huffingtonpost.com/2010/06/04/american-dad-horse-ejaculation-video_n_600231.html

Satanic Strategies

that have tipped the scales in favor of *immorality*. *The Simpsons* and *South Park* are two animated shows that leave no moral stone unturned. Whether it was Homer Simpson singing the praises of beer and alcohol, or Cartman from South Park swearing a blue street, or making toilet jokes, nothing is off limits.

The Simpsons was on for twenty-one years! That is a long time for any show, much less an animated one. The fact that it lasted as long as it did means that people were captured by the rankness of the humor, and the stupidity of the characters, along with many refer-

"Neighbors From Hell" centers on the Hellmans, a typical all-American suburban family with Balthazor; his wife, Tina; their two children, Mandy and Josh; and their dog, Pazuzu. They're your average family who happen to hail from Hell. They have been sent to Earth to pose as normal suburbanites with a mission to keep humans from drilling their way to Hell. Their task is made all the more complicated by Balthazor's growing affection for humans and their odd but endearing qualities, but as long as they follow Satan's acronym "Snorfindesdrillsalgoho" (Seem Normal, Fit In, Destroy Drill, Save Hell, Go Home), then the Hellmans have nothing to worry about. TBS began broadcasting this animated show in June of 2010.

ences to Freemasonry (The Stonecutters). That certainly says something about the crassness of society.

In the case of *South Park*, Jesus has been caricatured and most recently, the show attempted to caricature Muhammad, Islam's main prophet. In that case, Muslims around the world threatened death to Trey Parker and Matt Stone, the creators of the show. Attempting to avoid this situation, Comedy Central, the channel that airs the show, blurred the character of Muhammad out when the episode aired.

Neighbors from Hell, another animated show, this one from the TBS Network, has one family from hell coming to earth under Satan's orders, to keep humans from digging their way to hell. As this book was being written, the show had just started airing on TBS.

With the possible exception of *According to Jim*, it is difficult to think of a sitcom in which the husband/father is strong and in many ways, remains head of the home. Even here though, there was one episode that was completely uncharacteristic when the father/husband, played by Jim Belushi (brother of late John Belushi, of Saturday Night Live fame), sells his soul to the devil. It turns out to be only a dream, but the character of Satan (portrayed by James Lipton of Inside the Actor's Studio), was presented as a likeable, fair-minded devil, something he most certainly is not if the Bible has any truth to it.

We cannot turn the hands of time backwards. The days of innocence are gone forever. What we have upon us is nothing less than the unprecedented power of evil that undergirds the entertainment industry. We can expect more of the same, becoming even more offensive. It is not clear how that can possibly happen except to add 3-D to the mix, along with even better special effects, and more nudity and sex! It is all relative to what the current trends are based upon and of course, this is forced down the public's throat.

Relativism is the natural outflow of humanism. Humanism cannot have moral absolutes. It will not work if it does. In order for man to be fully elevated, he must first realize that there are no moral absolutes. There is no real right and wrong. It is only wrong for one person if that person believes it to be wrong.

Humanism and relativism go hand in hand and Satan has been working to reshape the areas of society so that they all feed into a form of humanistic relativism. Once he can successfully overturn God's absolutes, exchanging them for his *lack* of absolutes, then he has effectively created a society in which moral perversion is the norm.

Isn't this what Paul refers to in Romans chapter one? In that chapter, Paul discusses the trail that leads people to the point of becoming so debased, that they no longer *want* to have their conscious bothering them. In that case, God gives them over to their desires and their consciences become *seared*. They no longer feel a sense of shame when doing the things that God prohibits, because He knows what it does to the souls of humanity. People are then free to do whatever seems good to them in their own eyes.

Rather than elevating man, humanism with its accompanying relativism actually brings men to the point *lower* than animals. Animals live by *instinct*. Their decisions are often made for them because of their own particular nature. Housecats normally avoid water. They are normally drawn to mice and other small creatures they see in a field. Animals normally eat when they are hungry, not because they are bored, as humans do. The mating habits of animals are often different from one species to the next. Who taught them?

Instinct will keep an animal alive, unless they go up against an animal that is more intelligent, and one in which their instinct is greater than the instinct of the other animal. While humans *can* use instinct (often called a sixth sense or intuition), we normally make our decisions using rationale and logic. This is something that animals do not necessarily have access to because of the way they were created.

When human beings prefer to *ignore* conscience, they are actually making themselves more sordid and vulgar. They are removing from their decision-making process a key ingredient. Unfortunately, unlike animals, at that point, man becomes unable to do anything worthwhile, and just as the men during the days of Noah who continually thought only of evil, this is what people are becoming like in today's world. It is happening because people want desperately to ignore their consciences.

Multiple steps are involved in taking a person to this point, but they *will* get there if they insist on it. For those who do, society becomes the worse for it. For these people, there really is no going back. This is often the case with the über-rich. They have so much money that they do not know what to do with it, so they do whatever they want. This often involves the most outlandish and immoral things they can contrive.

Such is the life of the elite of this world, the people who believe they are above the law. As far as society is concerned, this may well be the case. As far as God is concerned, *no one* is above His Law, not one person or supernatural being.

SATANISM
Satanic Ritual Abuse (SRA)

Later on in this book, we will look at the subject of pedophile that shocks cities and nations. One of them took place in the country of Belgium in the 1990s. Religious Tolerance dot org, reporting on the Belgium case asks the question whether there were ties to Satanism, or what is known as *SRA* (Satanic Ritual Abuse).

For it be SRA, they believe there generally has to be at least three ingredients:

1. kidnapping of children

2. sexual abuse of children
3. confining victims in cages or dungeons

Though these things *were* present in the Belgium case, the writers on that particular Web site came to the conclusion that *"However, there is no indication from the scene, from the interviews of the two rescued victims, or from the confessions of the alleged perpetrators that any ritual abuse was involved - Satanic or otherwise."*[51]

They further point out, *"The entire operation appears to have been motivated by:*

"Young girls can be sold into prostitution for a great deal of money. Pornographic videotapes are easy to make and duplicate; they also can be sold for tremendous profit.

"Dutroux is a known pedophile who has continually acted out his perverted sexual attraction to young children, with no concern for their suffering

"But there appears to be no religious motivation for the abuse and confining of their victims. Belgium is not dealing with a case of Satanic ritual abuse here. The police have uncovered a criminal gang, not a religious cult."[52]

The writers also reference the so-called satanic panics of North America, noting that these turned out be "frauds" (their words). They point to individuals (referring to them as *"Evangelical Christian, Wiccan and secular investigators"*), whom they believe did the investigative work.

They emphasized the point with *"Many government studies in the United States, the Netherlands and the UK have concluded that abusing Satanic cults do not exist.* **No credible hard evidence of any such**

---

[51] http://www.religioustolerance.org/ra_charl.htm
[52] Ibid

abuse has surfaced, *in spite of great efforts by police forces over a 15 year period. The belief in Satanic abuse seems to have peaked in the late 1980's, and is now in decline in North America."*[53] (emphasis added).

The problem here is that this perspective seems to be naïve to say the least, based on the multitude of books, reporting, and even confessions by high-ranking Satanists. It seems to be the same old attitude that blames the person who believes they were abused. It smacks of when women are raped and rarely believed.

Incredibly, this same Web site makes these unbelievable statements:

"When the police and the rest of the public is presented with accounts of such incredible horror, they tend to suspend rational judgment. They never ask themselves logical questions. For example:

1. *how likely would the parents of a newborn child sell their infant to be sacrificed?*
2. *how could a cult member canvas couples with newborns without triggering a complaint to the police?*
3. *if many infants are abducted and sacrificed, how come their parents do not notice them missing and report the kidnapping?*
4. *why has a body of a sacrificed infant never been found in North America or Europe?"*[54]

Talk about suspending logic! Did it ever occur to these people that their *questions* suspend logic? Regarding question number one, we know that parents often (and unfortunately) sell their children in third world countries because of *economics*. It is tragic, but it happens.

---

[53] http://www.religioustolerance.org/ra_charl.htm
[54] Ibid

Do the authors of Religious Tolerance dot org actually believe that parents are *told* what will happen to their children? It seems as though this is what they believe. Can you see it? A Satanist comes to the door of a hut somewhere in outer Africa and asks if they have any children to sell because they are needed for a satanic sacrifice at Midnight. It is *absurd*.

The second question is also asinine. Why would a cult member bother canvassing parents at all? Wouldn't the cult member simply wait for an opportune time to *kidnap* the infant or small child, as has happened so many times throughout history to today?

Question number three is easy to answer, knowing what we know now. Many, if not all parents *do* notice their children missing. In some cases, the parents themselves are in collusion to sacrifice the child, as sad as that fact is to all of us.

Recently, on June 4, 2010, a seven year-old boy named Kyron Horman simply disappeared from his *school* in a suburban area of Portland, Oregon. There have been little by way of clues that the public has been made aware of and one blogger wrote, *"[The officials] made it appear as though they had a lead, but they couldn't give out any details. They also used the term, "isolated case", which leads to think that they know something very criticial to the case that they haven't yet told the press!"*[55]

One news blog related, *"On Sunday, authorities announced that the search and rescue operation had officially transformed into a criminal investigation after 10 days of searching with no sign of Kyron."*[56] What happened to Kyron? Obviously, *something* changed. At this point, no one knows, or at least are not saying. Until the facts come out, we are left to guess.

---

[55] http://momlogic.gather.com/viewArticle.action?articleId=281474978306259
[56] http://www.nwcn.com/news/Police-hope-billboards-small-clues-will-lead-to-Kyron-Horman-96475549.html

Regarding question number four (never finding the body of a sacrificed baby) from Religious Tolerance dot org, that one is the most outrageous. Again, it seriously appears as though these individuals have set logic and common sense on the shelf. It is as if they are wearing a sign that says, "*Hi. My brain is out to lunch.*"

In answer to the fourth question, it would be helpful to look at a few cases that will help to answer this question. It will answer the question with facts and details that they somehow have completely missed.

From the *Law Enforcement Examiner* comes an article by Jim Kouri titled, "*Satanic or ritualistic crime and murder.*"[57]

Jim writes on the murder of a 15 year-old woman named Elyse Marie Pahler in Southern California. He states that she, "*was 'sacrificed to Satan' by three San Luis Obispo, CA teen-agers in one of the most grisly murders on record.*"[58] Granted, Pahler was not a baby, but this crime occurred in 1996 and the parents of the young woman attempted to sue the band *Slayer* because the claimed that it was the band's music and lyrics that caused them to do what they did to their daughter.

For the record, according to one source Pahler, "*had been raped and murdered...by acquaintances Jacob Delashmutt, Joseph Fiorella and Royce Casey. The perpetrators apparently returned to the corpse and had sex with it on several occasions. The body was located after Casey confessed to the crime following a religious conversion to Christianity. All three eventually pleaded no contest to her murder and are now imprisoned and serving 25 years to life.*"[59]

---

[57] http://www.examiner.com/x-2684-Law-Enforcement-Examiner~y2009m4d14-Satanic-or-ritualistic-crime-and-murder
[58] Ibid
[59] http://en.wikipedia.org/wiki/Elyse_Pahler

Apparently, the men were in their own heavy metal band called, *Hatred* and told authorities they *"had lured Elyse from her house with the stated intention of killing her as part of a satanic ritual, although the crime bears many of the hallmarks of similar sexually motivated murders. In their defence [sic], the defendants said they had needed to commit a 'sacrifice to the devil' in order to give their heavy metal band, Hatred, the 'craziness' to 'go professional'. The trio choked and stabbed Elyse to death, later returning to have sex with her corpse."*[60]

Kouri notes, *"In spite of mankind's advances in the arts and sciences, there remain a number of people who have not been able to — or refuse to — shake-off the practices of pagan rituals, some of which date back thousands of years. Included within the broad spectrum of paganism are so-called Satanic cults which are suspect in a number of bizarre crimes throughout the United States.*

"According to investigative journalist and author Maury Terry, **there exists a network of Satan-worshiping cults with members crisscrossing our nation.** *Terry, whose research takes him to just about every state of the union, participated in a special regional police conference in Ohio, co-sponsored by the American Federation of Police and the National Association of Chiefs of Police."*[61] (emphasis added)

Kouri fully believes in the integrity of Terry and regarding Satanism, states, *"The world of the Satanic cultist is filled with ritualistic violence, perverse sexual activity and abuse, Heavy Metal music and the use of illegal drugs such as marijuana, amphetamines (crank, speed, meth, crystal), psilocybin (an hallucinogenic drug similar to LSD), heroin and other others. This is a world which, even in the beginning of the 21st Century, continues to attract a large number of young people*

---

[60] http://en.wikipedia.org/wiki/Elyse_Pahler
[61] http://www.examiner.com/x-2684-Law-Enforcement-Examiner~y2009m4d14-Satanic-or-ritualistic-crime-and-murder

who follow the precepts of Anton LaVey's Satanic Bible, a volume that has millions of copies in print today."[62]

In order for satanic groups to grow enough to become a force to be dealt with, they must have lots of *members*. Kouri notes, *"According to Ed Briggs, crime reporter for the Richmond Times-Dispatch ,* **Satanic cults seduce teenagers and young adults with sex and drugs and the promise of power over others**. *Also, involvement in this religion is the ultimate in rebellion against parental control, especially if the parents are religious Christians, Jews, Muslims, or part of any mainstream religious organization including Religious Satanism which is recognized by the federal government as a legitimate religion deserving of all privileges enjoyed by Christian, Jewish, Muslim, etc. churches and temples."*[63] (emphasis added)

Large Numbers of Satanists

Lieutenant Larry Jones of the Boise, ID Police Department offers his estimate on the number of Satanists in this country and what they do. *"'The adherents of this violent [quasi-]religion number over* **300,000**, *The kids become involved in sacrificial rituals, violent song lyrics, Satanic symbolism, suicide notes or recordings, all enhanced with illegal, mind-altering drugs, which play a major role [in the drama of a Black Mass]. And the added secrecy of the cult members makes estimating their numbers impossible.' says Detective Jerry Simandl, a veteran of the Chicago Police Department and assigned to the Gang Crime Task Force."*[64] (emphasis added)

While Kouri is careful to point out that not all practicing Satanists have a thirst for blood, the ones that do, often involve themselves in numerous rituals. *"During the course of these so-called religious rituals, drug use is usually rampant and heightens the frenzy and blood-*

---

[62] http://www.examiner.com/x-2684-Law-Enforcement-Examiner~y2009m4d14-Satanic-or-ritualistic-crime-and-murder
[63] Ibid
[64] Ibid

lust of the cultists. According to Pat Pulling, a criminologist who lectures police departments on the occult and Satanism, rituals may include:

- Victim is placed in a coffin or make-shift coffin.
- Paraphernalia and symbols such are pentagrams, 666 symbols, inverted crosses, etc.
- Heavy feeding of drugs, especially hallucinogens.
- Kidnapping victims.
- Sexual abuse aimed at confusing a recruit and destroying his/her moral foundation.
- Incestuous sex acts (family is involved in the cult).
- Animal or (rarely) human sacrifice.
- Cannibalism.
- Cremation (destruction of victim along with evidence)."[65]

Is this a good time to ask *again,* where the folks at Religious Tolerance dot org obtained their information? It appears as though their information does not gel with that of the real experts who have spent years studying this phenomenon.

Kouri's research has also led him to other conclusions about Satanists, the Black Mass, as well as infant sacrifice. *"During the Black Mass, at least as it's performed by self-styled Satanic groups, animal sacrifices are commonplace and sexual experimentation follows large doses of illegal drugs. Although there have been reports of human sacrifices, especially infanticide, these incidents are extremely rare.*

"Those claiming they are not rare but routine say that the infants used in the monstrous ceremony is one that has been conceived and raised just for the purpose of ritual murder. These police officers -- Sandi Gallant among them -- say that birth records of these babies do not exist

---

[65] http://www.examiner.com/x-2684-Law-Enforcement-Examiner~y2009m4d14-Satanic-or-ritualistic-crime-and-murder

since the children are born using midwife who's a member of the group or even a physician-member. Children born into a cult are called Generationals."[66]

Much of the information you have just read, provided by Jim Kouri, is ultimately from *law enforcement officials*, who see the results of these crimes. They deal with carcasses of dead animals, or in some cases, of human beings. They see the satanic paraphernalia at many crime scenes and catalog it.

If anyone understands what occurs in satanic crimes, it would be police officers and detectives whose sole responsibility in these situations is to determine exactly *what happened*. It should not be that difficult to believe that these events *are* taking place if numerous police officials are saying that they are taking place.

Kouri also points out that FBI *"Special Agent Robert Ressler, during his interviews with over 100 serial-killers and unusually violent criminals,* **found elements of the occult** *in the psyche of a few of these killers."*[67] (emphasis added)

The reality is that it does not matter if these people believe in an actual being named Satan. All that matters is that they believe in their own twisted way that the dark arts and the occult will give them what they crave. Because of that, they willingly participate in events where sacrifices take place, and at least in some cases, the actual crime of murder that they might participate in *is* the act of sacrifice. This needs to be understood in order to gain insight into how these people think.

With respect to those who become involved in aspects of Satanism, they are usually younger people and they become involved through a

---

[66] http://www.examiner.com/x-2684-Law-Enforcement-Examiner~y2009m4d14-Satanic-or-ritualistic-crime-and-murder
[67] Ibid

variety of means. According to the experts, involvement in Satanism comes through:

- "*so-called Black-Metal music, most successful being Venom. Some of the more popular bands such as Ozzy Osbourne (of Black Sabbath fame) may touch on Satan and evil, but they are entertainers, not cult recruiters).*
- *Fantasy role-playing in games such as Dungeons & Dragons. A surprisingly large number of homicides and suicides have been linked to D & D such as the Joseph Vite case in Kenosha, Wisconsin, and the Juan Kimbrough case in Oakland, California. Both were murdered as part of a game of D& D.*
- *An unhealthy obsession with movies, books and videos about Satanism and the Black Arts (witchcraft).*
- *Involvement with Satanists at a rock concert or party (college campuses are ripe for recruiters). The promise of sex and drugs is an attractive incentive.*
- *Involvement with classmates heavily into occult, Satanism or serious fantasy role-playing.*"[68]

Besides the aforementioned situation with Elyse Marie Pahler, many other groups have claimed to commit their heinous crimes *for* Satan, or *as* Satanists. It is difficult to understand why Religious Tolerance dot org seemed unable to uncover the same information that has been presented here. Can anyone forget Charles Manson, Satan-worshiper himself?

Ripper Crew
Does anyone recall a group known as the "Ripper Crew" from the 1990s who are said to have killed 18 prostitutes, sacrificing the women to Satan? "*In the early eighties Robin Getch, a former employee of John Wayne Gacy, and three associates, Edward Spreitzer and*

---

[68] http://www.examiner.com/x-2684-Law-Enforcement-Examiner~y2009m4d14-Satanic-or-ritualistic-crime-and-murder

brothers Andrew and Thomas Kokoraleis, had a Satanic cult suspected for the disappearances of 18 women in the streets of Chicago. Known as the Ripper Crew, Getch and his gang drove around in a van looking for prostitutes to sacrifice in Getch's apartment. They would remove one breast from each victim and eat it as Robin read passages of the bible."[69]

Another group referred to as the "Siberian Satanist Cult" is credited with five deaths in the late 1990s. *"Russian police announced that they were searching for the ringleaders of a Satanic cult in western Siberia. The cult is believed to be from the city of Tyumen, 1,400 miles east of Moscow, where five young people have been found hanged to death in what, at first, authorities thought were suicides. Later, the discovery of cabalistic jottings in the belongings of the dead youths revealed their involvement in a seven-stage initiation ceremony that culminated in ritual suffocation."*[70]

It should be noted that the individuals who killed themselves were all friends and routinely gathered in the basement of one of the friends. In the basement was a type of *"Satanic altar and had walls painted with diabolical signs and cryptic symbols."*[71]

This particular Web site lists twenty-two specific cases of crimes by admitted Satanists:
www.francesfarmersrevenge.com/stuff/serialkillers/satanism.htm

Not trying to be unnecessarily repetitive, but *where* did the folks at Religious Tolerance dot org get their information that enabled them to make declarative statements as they have done? It would appear that these folks are going strictly by *externals*. They seem unwilling or unable to look beneath the surface.

---

[69] http://www.mayhem.net/Crime/cults1.html
[70] Ibid
[71] Ibid

Unfortunately, this also occurs in areas of law enforcement as well when interviewing individuals that are thought to be connected to a crime. *"According to Detective Sandi Gallant of the San Francisco PD, there are many problems with investigation and prosecution of ritualistic crime cases...*

- *Investigators disregard original statements regarding rituals and Satanism; therefore detectives and officers only document the outward appearances of the crime such as sexual abuse.*
- *No physical evidence is found to substantiate statements given by victims or former cult members.*
- *Crime scenes are never found.*
- *Crime scenes are found, but do not fit the descriptions given.*
- *Crime victims are interviewed together in the presence of parents or legal guardians. They may be ashamed to discuss their victimization in front of them or they are terrified to discuss the case because their parents or guardians are part of the cult.*
- *The suspects and the news media become aware of the case prematurely.*
- *Because of the illegal drugs involved, it may be difficult for investigators to believe the statements made by victims or former cultists, especially when drugs such as LSD and psylosybin are involved.*
- *There is an inability to establish a corpus delecti ("body of the crime")*
- *Although murders are reported, no bodies are found (**Satanists believe in cremation**).*
- *Even though children claim they saw other children who were kidnapped, no record can be found with the National Center for Missing and Exploited Children or with the FBI.*

- *The prosecutor wishes to downplay the Satanic or occult nature of the crime in order to avoid problems with witness credibility, etc.*
- *The statements of victims and witnesses may appear outlandish and the reputation of the accused may appear impeccable."*[72] (emphasis added)

People Prefer NOT to Believe

There are any number of reasons why people do not generally believe in Satanic crimes. A few reasons have already been listed and the quote from Religious Tolerance dot org serves as a case in point. Detective Ray Parker indicates, *"Child abuse is difficult enough to deal with. One-on-one child abuse, Daddy does child or neighbor does child – that's hard. Juries don't like to face it. Nobody likes to face it."*[73] It becomes clear very quickly that people would rather deny the very real situation of child abuse. What is even easier to deny are the circumstances in which children are ritually abused in Satanic worship situations. That smacks of an evil from far back in humanity's history, something most prefer to believe is so distant that it no longer exists. *"Because of the nature of these allegations, many people don't believe the children's stories. That's not surprising. Children make poor witnesses in the eyes of the courts. Because these stories, though bizarre, are so similar to others around the country, however, officials are beginning to believe them."*[74]

Kahaner also points out from the numerous conversations he has had with those in law enforcement, that many of these children cannot read, yet can describe situations that allegedly occurred with *detail*. That and the fact that many children who are not connected to one another in any way, shape, or form, often share the same *type* of details about how they were ritually abused. This fact, coupled with

---

[72] http://www.mayhem.net/Crime/cults1.html
[73] Larry Kahaner *Cults That Kill* (Warner Books 1988), 199
[74] Ibid, 199

the amount of detail they are able to share, in spite of the fact that they could not have read it anywhere, provides greater credibility to their testimony, regardless of how they come across as a witness.

In one situation in San Francisco, a little boy named "Kevin" had turned up missing. A mother and her young daughter were watching the news when the girl stated simply, *"My daddy and I picked up a little boy named Kevin the other day and he looks like him."*[75] As it happens, the young girl's father was already being investigated for a sexual abuse case.

The mother became concerned because of all the things that the little girl was saying and wanted investigators to talk to her. The little girl was only *three years-old* at the time. The girl had undergone an emotional change recently, and her schoolwork was suffering and she had become much more introverted. Because of this and other emotional problems in evidence, the little girl's mother decided to take the girl to see a therapist.

A Little Girl's Experience
The girl chose to draw images to depict what she says she had seen. *"The pictures showed knives, swords, swastikas, pentagrams, people in robes, cries for help, and a child being thrown in a fire."*[76] This harkens back to the days of the Old Testament when the people would sacrifice their children to Molech by 'passing them through the fire,' (cf. 1 Kings 11:7; 2 Kings 23:10; Leviticus 18:21; 20:2-5; Jeremiah 32:35). This form of sacrifice was reprehensible because during the process, babies and young children were sacrificed by *parents* to Molech. The child was placed in the arms of the statue of Molech, often built with arms that would bend down toward the pit in front of him. It was in this pit that a huge bonfire would be created and as the arms of Molech came down holding the child, the child would fall

---
[75] Larry Kahaner *Cults That Kill* (Warner Books 1988), 202
[76] Ibid, 203

into the fire. Often a band of musicians would play their instruments loudly at this point to cover the screams of the unfortunate child.

It seems clear that modern Satanists taking their cue from Molech, either burn the body *during* their worship service, or dispose of it *later* using crematoriums. The little girl continued to draw details of what she had allegedly seen during the worship services she was forced to attend. *"On one occasion, a man came into the room and brought with him a baby. The baby is given an injection. There is a fire going in the fireplace. They put the baby's legs in the fire. We just let her tell the story, but I did stop her every once in a while to ask questions. At that point, I said, 'Did the baby make any noise?' She said, 'The baby screamed'."*[77]

The girl continued, drawing a picture of a knife that she said was used in the ritual. At one point, her *"father brought her a knife – she called it a knife and drew it for us. It looked like a dagger in her drawing. She drew the whole scenario for us in fact. Her father gave her the knife and told her to put it in the baby's belly. She wouldn't do it. Her father got behind her and put his hand over hers and put it into the belly. I asked her, 'What happened next?' She said, 'I saw worms come out'."*[78]

It turns out that what the little girl had described may very well have been the baby's *intestines*. Even though it was difficult for these hardened detectives to believe, they felt an obligation to investigate. Over time, something became clear with nearly all of these types of stories they were hearing. *"One universal story, something almost all of them talk about, is cooking the baby. This is one story that goes throughout. I make it a point not to ask them direct questions. I try to be real sensitive with the kids. They usually begin talking about cook-*

---

[77] Larry Kahaner *Cults That Kill* (Warner Books 1988), 205
[78] Ibid, 205

Below: An 18th century illustration of Molech and child sacrifice.

ing the baby, boiling the baby, or cooking body parts. This is the thing that made me believe."[79]

It appears that for Satanists, ritual killing of animals and even babies is part of their worship *of* and *to* Satan. Whether they believe in an actual being called, Satan is totally beside the point. They obviously believe in some power that they can tap into or direct when they follow prescribed rituals. Many to most of these rituals include sacrificial death. One woman, who had grown up in a satanic cult relates,

---

[79] Larry Kahaner *Cults That Kill* (Warner Books 1988), 227

Satanic Strategies

"Some of the ceremonies would be performed to gain Satan's power through the terror of the child. The child would be starved, tortured, and raped in order to gain that power. Some of the ceremonies were strictly for sacrificial killings for Satan. The child would be killed with a knife through the heart while a cult member was raping the child. The point of all this was to have the sexual climax at the point of death of the child. The terror of the child and the sexual climax seemed to give the ultimate in control and power and this power was supposed to come from Satan."[80]

Getting Rid of the Remains

This same woman explains how the bodies used in these sacrifices were disposed of by the members. *"The bodies were always burned. Some of the bones were kept as implements for the ceremonies. I have one memory of a place where we lived in Denver where there were certain places in the backyard where I was not permitted to play. I vaguely have a memory that some bones were buried there."*[81]

Of course, opponents have come forward to not only question any and all of these narratives, but to completely discredit the individual making the claims. Certainly, it is wise to question the validity of these claims, or what people call "recovered memories" because they may either be completely false, or inaccurate to some degree.

This has led to what is termed the "False Memory Syndrome," coined by the False Memory Syndrome Foundation. Groups so-named believe it their job to not only disprove what has been reported, but in many cases, go further in discrediting the person making the claims. "'However, despite its scientific sounding title, there is no clinically acknowledged 'false memory syndrome' at this time, said Judith Herman, M.D., an associate clinical professor of psychiatry at Harvard Medical School, and author of Trauma and Recovery. 'The very name FMSF is

---

[80] Larry Kahaner *Cults That Kill* (Warner Books 1988), 232-233
[81] Ibid, 233

prejudicial and misleading,' said Herman. 'There is no such syndrome, and we have no evidence that reported memories are false. We know only that they are disputed'."[82]

Apparently, there are some inconsistencies within the FMSF. "Besides accused parents, FMSF has been able to enlist some professionals to function as spokespeople to the media, to serve as 'expert' trial witnesses, and so on. However, some apparent ironies have surfaced in connection with the FMSF organization.

"The following is an excerpt from a February 29, 1992, FMSF Newsletter where the organization claims it is:

> **'...not in the business of representing pedophiles...We are a good looking bunch of people: graying hair, well-dressed, healthy and smiling...Just about every person is someone you would likely find interesting and want to count as a friend'.**"[83]

There is at least one record pertaining to one of these "experts" in which the individual (Dr. Leo Pilo), pled guilty to *pedophilia*. Though his license to practice medicine was revoked, in a civil case brought by one of the doctor's victims, the fact that he had pled guilty and nothing related to the evidence of his pedophilia were allowed as part of that case.

Eventually, Dr. Pilo recanted his guilty plea and 'experts' came forward to claim that the victim likely suffered from False Memory Syndrome. There are a number of situations in which pedophiles, though vilified by the public, were treated as though they had done nothing wrong by 'professionals' in the field who came to their judicial aid.

---

[82] Daniel Ryder *Cover-Up of the Century* (Ryder Publishing 1994), 39-40
[83] Ibid, 40

Claims of Satanic Ritual Abuse have taken a bad rap, partly because it is so unbelievable to the average individual, and partly because those who are themselves perverted, often rise up to proclaim SRA to be the result of delusions. In many cases, it has been passed off as essentially urban legend.

In spite of what some individuals would like the public to believe (that SRA in actuality does not exist), the evidence is becoming more clear from state to state, across the nation, and the world.

It would seem then that in order to protect this vast conspiracy of Satanic Ritual Abuse and pedophilia, a growing complexity of protectors have arisen in order to act as a buffer between the public and the perpetrators of these acts.

7

SATANISM
PEDOPHILIA

Satanism, drugs, extreme versions of heavy metal or death music, pedophilia (sex with children), and other sexual perversions appear to have some type of connection in many cases. In fact, it is becoming so well known, and documented by numerous individuals throughout the world that it can no longer be denied. Those who attempt to deny it will only wind up looking like fools and they deserve to be viewed as such. Kahaner notes *"Satanism always flourishes during times of cultural decadence, when decadence is in fa-*

shion, when you have a particular ruling class in a country that feels threatened or is being besieged by new economic classes to where they're losing their prestige and political authority. The period between the world wars in England was a time of social experimentation, a period of nihilism. The ruling class in England had lost its taste for rule; it was a period of outraged scandal and decadence. Occultists like Crowley flourished in that time."[84]

Worldwide in Scope

David Icke has done years of research and has come to some very disturbing conclusions. In an electronic newsletter article, he wrote in March of 2010, he highlights some very disturbing statistics. He opens his article with these ominous and frightening words:

Shown above is one of the universal symbols used by pedophiles to attract little girls and boys.

"I have had countless surprises and many shocks as I have lifted the stone and seen what horrors lie beneath, but few more than the scale of child abuse and Satanism.

"And that's the word - **scale**. The fact that it is happening is one thing, but to realise (sic) how widespread and fundamental it is to establishment power all over the world was truly shocking.

"I have talked with people in the best part of 50 countries in my research of this subject, the abused, the insiders who know the abusers, and those who have dedicated their lives to exposing this evil."[85]

---

[84] Larry Kahaner *Cults That Kill* (Warner Books, 1988), 59

[85] http://www.davidicke.com/articles/child-abuse-mainmenu-74/31148-paedophilia-and-satanism--the-fabric-of-the-web

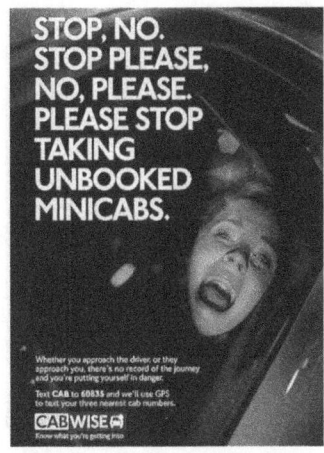

Left: A public service ad warning of the dangers of riding in unbooked cabs. It could mean a child's life.

In the 1980s, while the Passantinos and other staff writers from *Cornerstone Magazine* were busy doing their level best to hit the delete button on the idea that people were being abused, tortured, and even killed in the name of Satanism, it obviously *existed* then. It did not simply spring up overnight since 2008 or later. It has been here all along, destroying lives, and capturing souls.

The evidence is becoming too difficult to ignore and even in their best efforts, no authentic journalist would be able to take no notice of the evidence that exists today for the reality of Satanism. No journalist worth his or her salt would even attempt to do so. What they would likely do is simply *disregard* all that is happening in the world with respect to Satanism and the occult.

Obviously, times have changed. It seems to have gotten to a point where even though it can be proven that these secret underground situations exist with the abuse of children, it also seems as though people have become hardened to that reality. While they might be willing to admit that it occurs, they seem to unwilling (or unable) to do more than shake their heads while noting how tragic it is that it happens. The overall situation appears to be overwhelming, making it difficult for the average individual to fully grasp the situation without feeling as if they are completely powerless to do anything to rectify it.

Had this been allowed to remain on the surface when it was first brought to the attention of the public years ago, things might be different *now*. Unfortunately, we do not have the luxury of wishful

Right: An illustration purporting to show Prophet Muhammad and his child-bride, 9 year-old Aisha

thinking, because the past is past. The only thing we can do now is *acknowledge* that it exists, learn as much as we can about it, and work to not only keep it from getting worse, but also work to undo what is taking place in today's world one life at a time.

We all know that pedophiles are individuals who prefer to have sexual relations with children. Often simply called *child molesters*, these individuals are found within many families and often have a natural rapport with children. *"They can be parents. They can be surgeons. They can be holy men. They can literally be anyone, and that is why they are so difficult to spot."*[86]

It is clear from the many filed cases that pedophiles may start by *wanting* to have sex with children. However, that becomes very boring and so they may go from that to murder. Once they murder, they begin fantasizing about ways to torture *before* they murder.

Satanism and Pedophilia

Icke continues, *"Put it all together and the situation is as clear as can be: paedophilia (sic) and Satanism are the cement that hold the establishment control structure together in every country, and these 'national' networks connect together to form a global network of paedophiles and Satanists all watching each others' backs - while they continue to serve the Control System."*[87]

---

[86] Dr. Deborah Schurman-Kauflin *Vulture Profiling Sadistic Serial Killers* (Universal Publishers 2005), 91

[87] http://www.davidicke.com/articles/child-abuse-mainmenu-74/31148-paedophilia-and-satanism--the-fabric-of-the-web

According to Icke, pedophilia is the glue that keeps everyone connected to the network. In other words, pedophilia is the source that can be used as blackmail against those who want to get out and stop doing what they are doing *with* and *against* children. It is not uncommon for pedophiles who become murderers to have some connection with the occult, even if only with a fringe-type association.

He elaborates further by noting, "***If anyone wants to get out or refuses to take orders they know the consequences - 'suicide' or exposure.*** *Governments around the world are being controlled by the bloodline cabal via paedophile and Satanist politicians and 'leaders' who dare not resist the demands of the Shadow People who have the evidence that would destroy them.*"[88] (emphasis added)

Icke provides support for his claims as well, support that the "investigative journalists" of the 1970s and 80s would not be able to discount, try as they might. *"A few weeks ago a document came to light in Australia purporting to be a 'death bed confession' by a leading Satanist from the 'top' coven/lodge in Sydney. It certainly rang true because what it said is supported by my 15 years research into these matters. It said:*

"'Politicians are introduced by a carefully graded set of criteria and situations that enable them to accept that their victims will be, 'Our little secret.' Young children sexually molested and physically abused by politicians worldwide are quickly used as sacrifices. In Australia the bodies are hardly ever discovered, for Australia is still a wilderness'."[89]

How many times have you read or heard someone say something like, "*Oh come on, if Satanism and ritual sacrifices were that prevalent, where are the bodies?*" They believe that this one question settles the

---

[88] http://www.davidicke.com/articles/child-abuse-mainmenu-74/31148-paedophilia-and-satanism--the-fabric-of-the-web
[89] Ibid

matter rhetorically. Unfortunately, they are not thinking outside of the box. In fact, they are not even thinking *logically*.

IF Satanism with its connection to animal and human sacrificial killings *does* exist in our day, does anyone actually believe that these Satanists would *not* have plans in place to eliminate the remainders of any humans used in sacrifices? It is absurd to think that this would not be taken into account by working it out ahead of time.

Bodies Disappear One Way or Another
Icke offers one possibility for the fact that bodies are rarely if ever found. *"In more crowded locations the Satanists and paedophiles (sic) (the two networks are fundamentally connected) have crematoria to 'lose' the evidence of child sacrifice and murder."*[90]

So besides bodies simply being dumped in wilderness areas of Australia for instance, it is possible that Satanists have access to crematoriums to make disposal of bodies that much easier. How hard is this to believe? No person who commits a brutal crime as murder ever wants to be caught. In fact, there are many unsolved cases where the only "evidence" is the fact that someone is *missing* and has never been located. What has happened to all of the people who are nowhere to be found? They must be *somewhere* if they are alive. If they are *not* alive, they are still *somewhere*, even if it is in a pile of ashes in a remote place.

Moreover, if bodies of humans sacrificed to Satan are dumped in areas of wilderness, how long would the body last before some wild animal, or a group of them happened upon the body? Once discovered, the animals would devour it, leaving nothing left for discovery. Why is this difficult to believe for some?

---

[90] http://www.davidicke.com/articles/child-abuse-mainmenu-74/31148-paedophilia-and-satanism--the-fabric-of-the-web

The major reason it is difficult to believe has everything to do with the fact that people believe human beings throughout the world are *civilized*, for the most part. Civilized people do not sacrifice *babies*, young adults, and older adults to Satan. It just does not happen, they reason. While it *may* take place in areas of the world in which Third World countries live by superstitions and medicine is still in the care of the tribal witch doctor, the rest of the world is safe from this type of crime. Is it?

Modern Day Molech Sacrifices: *Abortion*
Most women who have one abortion have less difficulty having another. While they may certainly not believe that they are sacrificing their children to Satan, it is clear that they are *killing* their children because having a child *inconveniences* them. While it is shouted from the rooftops that women should have total control over their bodies, one would think that total control would start *before* one gets pregnant, not afterwards.

The slaughter of millions of babies every year is nothing less than murder. Satan delights in this because he is causing human beings to take the lives of other human beings. It would appear that at least one of the reasons why abortion will remain legal until our Lord comes has to do with the elite of this world. They have concluded that there are excessively many people on this planet, so a percentage needs to *die*.

Abortion serves their purpose and so does euthanasia. While not legal yet, it could very well be in the coming years. Some people have gone so far to believe that our government is slowly killing us with what they term "chemtrails." These are found within jet streams in the skies, which (they believe) is the release of chemicals into the breathable atmosphere. Over time, these chemicals will cause untold illnesses and early death. Is it true? Who knows, but with the way things are going these days, it would not surprise this author to discover that it is in fact, true.

It has also come to be common knowledge that throughout the world, the sex trade is alive and well. There is documented evidence that it exists and documentaries on this subject offer the proof. Women, who have either been kidnapped, or answered an ad for a job in numerous foreign countries, have walked into their worst nightmare, and to their additional horror, are unable to extricate themselves. They are quickly overcome and forced into prostitution. There is no getting out for most of them either, at least alive. We know this exists and that it is despicable. Most of us also feel completely helpless to do anything for the release of the women caught in the web of this satanic holocaust.

If the sex trade is alive, then why not kidnapping for the purposes of ritual killing? Is it so difficult to believe? If so, it may be because of the western *mindset*. Part of the problem has to do with exactly *how much* of this type of abuse, sadism, pedophilia, and the rest occurs throughout the world. The other part of the equation has to do with the very reason *why* these events are occurring. What is behind them, the reason for them? There is a motive that causes people to do anything. Why would people feel the need or desire to do things that bring harm to themselves or others?

Satanic Killings

In 1989, Texas University student Mark Kilroy went to Brownsville, Texas and then onto Matamoros, Mexico with some friends over Spring Break. It was during this time that Kilroy became separated from his friends briefly and was never seen alive again.

It was not until weeks later, when Mexican Police raided a farm after following a suspected drug runner, did they discover more than they bargained for in a storage shed on the property. *"Authorities also discovered an assortment of 'voodoo paraphernalia,' a blood splattered altar of sacrifice, cheap rum, human body parts, animal bones, chicken and goat heads, as well as the witch's cauldron filled with the foul mixture of blood and flesh."*[91]

As the search continued on the property, Mexican officials also uncovered a common grave in which 15 individuals were buried. It was discovered that the most recent victim was Mark Kilroy. As it turns out, this had been the work of an extreme branch of *Santería*, a religion steeped in the *occult, voodoo,* and *superstition*. These cults take their religion very seriously.

As stated, there is always a reason why people do anything, and in this case, the main purpose for offering these human sacrifices seems to be related to *drugs*. *"The bodies of dozens of people were found mutilated and sacrificed in occult rituals used for blessings over drug manufacturing."*[92]

Remember, this took place in 1989, some eleven years *after* Mike Warnke's book, *The Satan Seller,* was published and just three year *prior* to the publication of Lauren Stratford's book, *Satan's Underground: The Extraordinary Story of One Woman's Escape*. *"Authorities also discovered an assortment of "voodoo paraphernalia," a blood splattered altar of sacrifice, cheap rum, human body parts, animal bones, chicken and goat heads, as well as the witch's cauldron filled with the foul mixture of blood and flesh.*

"The human sacrifices offered to Satan were people who were abducted off of the streets, locals and otherwise. Tapia sheds some light on those who performed homage by human sacrifice to their god."[93]

Prior to and even after the Matamoros discovery, the idea of Satanism and Satanists actually torturing, killing, and dismembering their

---

[91] http://www.angelfire.com/electronic2/kc_jones/004.HTM
[92] Ibid
[93] Ibid

victims as a sacrifice to Satan was thought to be absurd. Though the Matamoros situation was real, it must have been an isolated event.

Just the mention of it with a serious expression would be enough to warrant a call to the people who carry straightjackets and take their guests on a one-way trip to a rubber room. The whole subject was off-limits for any serious, intelligent person.

Satanism was often thought to be the result of overworked imaginations of Christian *fundamentalists*, who saw skeletons, ghosts, goblins, and devils around every corner and in every closet. Those people were still living in the middle ages and had never gotten beyond that time when imaginations ran wild, as did accusations.

However, the grisly discovery of 15 bodies at a ranch in Matamoros *began* to strip away the unbelief. People were cautious about how widespread this act had been. Was it merely an incident by one group of aberrant individuals who took their religion to the extreme, or were there more of the same throughout Mexico as well as other parts of the world? However, even with this, when Lauren Stratford's book came out a few years *later*, the Passantinos went after her with a vengeance.

They were not alone, as our friends at Religious Tolerance dot org have this to say about that incident: *"In early 1989, the bodies of over a dozen murdered men were found in Matamoros, Mexico, close to the Texas border. A media frenzy resulted in which the killings were blamed on Satanists, Witches, Voodoo priests, and/or Santerians. Everybody seemed to have a different theory. After the lurid headlines died down and the police investigation concluded, the murderers were found to be orchestrated by an individual hired by a criminal gang of drug runners in order to obtain protection from the police for the gang members. The gang members happened to be followers of a variety of religious groups common to the area including Christianity, Palo Mayombe and Santeria. But no link was ever found between their faith and their drug running or murderous practices. The immediate cause of the murders was the gang leader's requirement that the members watch a Hollywood movie called The Believers a total of 14 times. That movie took elements of the Santerian faith, and added concepts foreign to the religion, including human sacrifice. If a single influencing cause needs to be assigned to the murder, it should be that movie."*[94] Thank goodness the level-headed folks at Religious Tolerance dot org *really* know what's going on and all the rest of us just run around like chickens with our heads cut off! In one swell swoop, they removed Satan from these situations, in spite of what the perpetrators themselves had to say. The drug runners *believe* that sacrificing to Satan gives them power and protection.

Regarding the Matamoros incident, Carl Raschke points out, *"Not only were the bodies themselves visible to an international television audience, the cultists' own confessions were trotted out in detail to legions of journalists from both sides of the border, primarily because of the coercive character of the Mexican judicial system and a hard-driving, publicity-seeking Matamoros police commander. In effect, the distasteful episode was dissected with probably more intimacy and interest than the Charles Manson murders in California almost a generation earlier."*[95]

Lest we think that this particular, religious group is an abnormality we need to realize that these types of groups are popping up all over the United States. *"A full-time crew for the Metro-Dade Department of Public Works pulls garbage from the Miami River every day by the ton, much of it related to rituals. In a three-month period in 1989, the crew removed two hundred decapitated (but not plucked) chickens; twenty-two similarly headless ducks; and an assortment of eels, iguanas, pelicans, pigeons, snakes, turtles, cats, and dogs -- beheaded or marked in ways consistent with Palo Mayombe and Santeria. One day,*

---

[94] http://www.religioustolerance.org/santeri1.htm
[95] Carl A. Raschke *Painted Black* (Harper and Row, 1990), 3

a calf's head turned up in a nearby canal with its brain removed. Later, a headless goat was found floating next to a murdered drug trafficker-- the Santero's way of paying for taking a life by offering another to the orishas."[96]

Of course, Religious Tolerance dot org has something to say about that situation as well. *"Many individuals and groups who attempt to raise public awareness [about] Ritual Abuse or of Satanic Ritual Abuse often mistakenly use these killings as evidence of human sacrifice by religious minorities.* **Ritual abuse and murder does exist***, and there are many dead bodies to prove it. But instances to date have had no connection with Santeria or any other small faith group. Most of the deaths have been caused by unintentional murder during Christian exorcisms."*[97] (emphasis added) Here at least, they are admitting that these crimes *do* take place (which seems to contradict their previously stated position), but their reasoning still seems off, if compared to law enforcement information.

Satanism and Drugs Equals Money and Power
What is also notable is the connection between many of these groups and the drug trade. If not for the drug trade between Mexico and the United States as well as other countries who illegally smuggle their drugs into this country, there would be little need for the type of ritualistic killings and sacrifices that take place.

In essence, modern day Satanism is a play for *power*, *protection*, and *greater wealth* by criminals. Not all Satanists believe in a real devil. Some deny that God or Satan exist at all. Others believe fully that Satan exists and that he is the *real* god, not Jehovah of the Bible.

In the case of the Mark Kilroy situation, the main players under leader Adolfo de Jesus Constanzo, all wanted this type of power that they believed came from torture-killings. Many of these individuals be-

---

[96] http://www.angelfire.com/electronic2/kc_jones/004.HTM
[97] http://www.religioustolerance.org/santeri1.htm

lieve that the greater the torture, the greater the power. *"In Mexican **brujeria,** or black magic, abject torture is a strategic ploy to capture the soul of an enemy or victim. The soul of the victim is taught through the ordeal to fear the murderer completely and for eternity. At the same time, the 'energy' from the pain and fear of the victim is appropriated sacramentally by the torturer in order to enhance his magical strength and theoretically his soul. The idea is a very primitive one, but Satanism has always been a return to archaic psychology in some sense."*[98]

This is the tragedy. Whether or not people *believe* that they are worshiping Satan is actually besides the issue. The fact that they believe they are gaining some spiritual significance from these brutal acts is all they need to convince themselves that the acts themselves are worth committing.

For the drug smuggler, or the leader of a drug cartel, they will do what they need to do to become more powerful than law enforcement and other drug smugglers. Drug smuggling is probably the biggest industry on the planet (except possibly prostitution), and of course one of the most dangerous. If a drug smuggler believes that sacrificing a human being will provide him with more power, strength, invincibility, or even the ability to become *invisible* (yes, invisible), then they will do what they need to do.

Tortured for Satan
According to Raschke, one of the favored means of torture by Satanists is *flaying* the victim alive. Who today has the temerity to say that none of this is related to Satanism? The plain fact of the matter is that *the dark lord promotes everything of this type of nature* because it satiates certain individuals, who are drawn to this type of sadism. Whether he somehow causes people to worship him directly or indirectly is not the point at all. The fact that people around the world

---

[98] Carl A. Raschke *Painted Black* (Harper and Row, 1990), 16

are involved in all sorts of sadistic, nefarious, acts perpetrated on other human beings and animals could have come from no other source, than Satan.

In the case of people who *want* more than anything to amass wealth and with it power, they will torture, kill or both in pursuit of that vision if they are already involved in criminal activities like drugs from the start.

If it is not drugs, then there are those who find prostitution more to their liking. However, we must realize that the people who are involved in either camp, are sadistic to a fault, and exercise absolutely no remorse at all when involving themselves in these heinous acts. They come to the point where they are completely hardened to the point that they have no heart for their victims. Either they are usually completely oblivious to their victims' screams of pain and terror, or they become (sexually) *excited* by them. If the latter, it has to do with the fact that they firmly believe themselves to be a god, in which they are the *master* of that person, deciding when that person will *die*. That heady experience produces within these individuals a sense of absolute power, making them feel insuperable.

This has turned out to be the situation in criminal cases of serial murder. These individuals often believe themselves to be deity in a human body. They control the situation. They control their victims. They make the decisions as to how, when, and where their victim will suffer and die. In the case of prostitution rings throughout the world, or the selling of young children and woman to the ultra-rich, the reality is much the same. It creates a sense of deity within the people who control these cartels. They are the ones who decide who lives, who dies, and how much a woman is sold for to another.

Satan's Desire
All of this stems from Satan's desire (and *promise to himself*) that he would ascend his throne *higher* than God's throne. Satan has always

wanted worship and for him, anything anti-God *is* worship because it involves people following Satan's path in manifesting every evil under the sun, instead of seeking and following God.

In the case of those individuals who are so rich, they can buy the world ten times over, many of these people are *bored*. Because they are bored *and fallen*, they find themselves seeking out things that are beyond the norm. Whether it is buying an island and castle, or whether it is eating some exotic animal that is illegal, these people believe they are completely above the law. This is because of all the money they have at their disposal. Their money brings them power. Because they have power, they are convinced they remain *untouchable* and that is often the case, at least in this life.

Their boredom often causes them to investigate the seamier side of life and once they go down that path, they normally follow it to the end. In the 1999 movie "Eyes Wide Shut," starring Tom Cruise and then-wife, Nicole Kidman (and directed by 33rd Degree Mason Stanley Kubrick), Cruise's character travels *"into a world of wealthy sex play at a masked ball of hedonism, [which] threatens his life, his self-respect, and his marriage."*[99] This is what the wealthy often do for kicks, because they can.

This is the problem with humanity. People, who do not follow God, *are* following Satan and he does not care how he causes people to follow him. He has people following him by default as soon as they are born since all people possess the sin nature and are therefore fallen beings in *need* of God's salvation.

In many cases, as pointed out by David Icke earlier, once people become involved in these situations, it is almost impossible for them to get out because of the potential for blackmail, or death. The path Satan sets before people leads ultimately to death.

---

[99] http://www.imdb.com/title/tt0120663/plotsummary

For many people involved in Satanism, the belief in an individual known as Satan does not even matter. All that matters is that they believe they are using the dark arts to achieve their own purposes. They believe in the *magic*, or the *supernatural*.

Passage to a Supernatural World

In the case of people involved in Freemasonry, it is the exact same thing. It is not a prerequisite that these people believe in a *real* devil. They may or may not. What matters is that they believe in the *dark arts*, which grant them passage to a supernatural world in which they believe they learn to fully control their own destiny.

For those who are super wealthy, and who involve themselves in sexual situations that are beyond the norm, they do not necessarily do this because they believe in Satan. They do not believe that abusing children or raping women is a form of sacrifice, or ritual. In many cases, that does not even matter. What matters is that they firmly believe themselves to be so far above the law, that they *are* gods. Because they have become gods, the laws of the land do not encumber them, for those laws are only for the lower class people.

Satanism takes many forms and much of it requires no belief in an actual being. In fact, Satan prefers to remain hidden from view so that people are not freaked by the fact that he truly exists. He would rather be in the shadows, sometimes showing himself as a benevolent higher or ascended master. At other times, he is a highly intelligent alien, bringing light to this earth. Still at other times, he is simply part of the "God" collective to many within the New Age Movement.

Only in certain occasions does he reveal himself as a dark lord, but even there, he does not allow his true malevolence to be seen, because people would die of fright. He needs to veil much of his wickedness, or at least redirect it so that the person he has under his spell never becomes aware of his true nature.

While Satan may *live* through a person causing them to do terrible things, that person may remain sealed off from experiencing the same type of abject terror that he instills in his victims. Of course, when we refer to Satan here, we are often referring to his underlings. Satan is saving himself for his own future "son," one named Antichrist. He will be the epitome of Satan in the flesh so that all the earth will marvel after the Antichrist. Even here, the Antichrist will not fully reveal his father Satan, until at least halfway into the Tribulation, when it becomes the *Great* Tribulation.

We must become aware of the biblical facts here. Satan has always meant to *deceive* people. He will not show his true nature because that will "burst" the bubble. Even for those who actually worship a being named Satan, he pretends to be benevolent *to them*. He allows them to believe that he means no harm to them at all, but has come to *give them power*.

This is the root of all of it. People want *power* and that specific form of power is different for each individual. Some find power through drugs or other illegal activities like prostitution. Others find power through what might be termed "old" money, money that has been in families for generations, inherited and passed down through generations. It is through many of those families that the Illuminati began and gained an interminable hold on society.

SATANISM
Sexual Perversion

There is a great deal of sexual perversion in the world today. Because of it, normal, heterosexual relationships are quickly becoming a joke. Timothy Leary's mantra *Tune In, Turn On, and Drop Out* could easily apply to this area, as it does to the drug culture.

Sadism, binding, masochistic fantasies, bestiality, and role-playing, and numerous other mindsets are quickly becoming the controlling force within sexual relations. The more perverse sex becomes, the better for many people.

Homosexuality has become a hot button for most politicians these days. It is difficult to be elected or re-elected unless you are willing to promise to help same-sex marriage become *legal*. It is also quickly becoming politically *incorrect* to say or even suggest that homosexuality is wrong, based on biblical standards.

Not only do people not want to hear this, but there have been and continue to be efforts to make it *illegal* to share that opinion with others in public discourse. To indicate a disagreement with the homosexual position may wind up being offensive, if a homosexual or a person who supports the homosexual agenda is in earshot. This could then become the catalyst that sends a person to prison, as has been the case in both England and Canada.

What is it homosexuals want? Ultimately, they want to be seen as *normal* by everyone. They want to be able to walk down the streets holding hands with their partner, or kissing them, without fear of reprisal. They want everything they do between themselves to be viewed no differently, than when the same things occur between heterosexual couples.

Certainly, this is asking a lot, especially from those of us who fully believe that God has specifically stated that homosexuality is *wrong* in a number of places in His Word. This does not matter to Gay and Lesbian groups though. They believe they should be free from verbal assault (which as stated, could simply mean hearing someone give their opinion that homosexuality is *wrong*).

In such a case, certainly the apostle Paul would have been thrown in prison for writing the first chapter of Romans. We have no record of Jesus condemning the act of homosexuality, but we *do* have Him referencing the situation with respect to Lot and Sodom and Gomorrah. Obviously, Jesus knew the event of the destruction of these two cities actually occurred. He shows no sign of believing that the narrative of Lot was merely *allegory*.

It is here though when things begin to heat up, because on one side of the aisle, there are the Gay individuals who do their best to explain away what *really* happened in Sodom and Gomorrah, and apparently, it had to do with a lack of hospitality on the part of the Sodomites. Of course, this flies in the face of the fact that Lot, not knowing what else to do, offered his virgin daughters to the men who wanted to "rape" the two angels who had arrived in the city to escort Lot and his family to safety.

If the problem was not homosexuality, then there was no reason at all for Lot to offer his daughters, in the hopes that they would at least turn away from the sin of sodomy. Of course, as stated, Lot did not really know what else to do, but he should *not* have offered his daughters. Fortunately for both Lot *and* his daughters, the homosexual men of the city were not the slightest bit interested in having sexual relations with Lots' daughters, which of course proves that the issue is homosexuality. They were more interested in raping the two angels, which is why they told Lot to send them out, that they "might know them." Due to the context, the word translated "know" here has the meaning of knowing as in having *sexual relations* with someone. It does not mean simply having a conversation with them, and thereby getting to know them.

Other Gay, Lesbian, and Transgender groups insist that what the men of Sodom wanted to do *was* to know them sexually. However, they want us to believe that this was apparently a *custom* among certain groups in those days (besides homosexuals, I cannot think of any other group that might be interested in this type of custom), and the two angels, not being from Sodom or Gomorrah, would not have been aware of that particular custom.

It is rather interesting when stopping to consider the absolute absurd way the Gay Community has tried to explain this situation. It is clear – if Scripture is allowed to speak for itself – the men wanted to gang rape two angels. That was their intent, their heart's desire, and their sexual proclivity. It was this type of heinous behavior that condemned the men of Sodom. God was left with no choice but to extinguish all life in those two cities, because they had allowed themselves to turn what God had instituted (marriage between one man and one woman) into a license to sin, man with man, *sexually*. It makes little sense at all, but there it is, out in the open, so to speak.

So what does this have to do with the coming New World Order? At least two things that we need to be aware of here. First, homosexuals do not *procreate*. If they are going to have children, they normally *adopt*. There are certainly cases of one person from same-sex couples either becoming pregnant (if a woman) from an in vitro fertilization procedure, or in the case of two men, one might donate sperm to a surrogate who, after giving birth, would give the child up to same-sex couples as previously agreed. Second, the New World Order is intent on designing their own moral code, which is more like a movable feast. For the elite leaders of the coming one-world order, morals are *not* absolute. In fact, there are no absolutes (unless handed down by the elite leadership of the one-world order), and what might be right for one person, may be wrong for another. It is the age old moral relativity problem. One day, for a short period of time, moral absolutes will no longer be in place.

Homosexuality is with us to *stay*. There will absolutely come a time when it is likely that the only countries that have not legalized same-sex marriage are those that have Sharia Law, which are Islamic countries. However, in a one-world order, Sharia Law (which goes against the idea of moral relativism), would have a difficult time existing, or being the law of the land. It is possible that these types of countries will be allowed (for a time) to control their citizenry with the tenets of Sharia Law. However, all civilized countries will adopt the mentality that says there is nothing at all wrong with same-sex marriage and should be universally allowed and even encouraged.

The legalization of same-sex marriage is merely another notch on the enemy's belt, which allows him to *replace* God's Law, with his own set of standards. Satan's standards are designed to uplift and glorify himself, all the while slapping God in the face. Of course, the reality is that God will no sooner be slapped in the face from these types of situations, as He was when He was crucified in Jesus Christ.

As this chapter is being written, it was reported that Iceland passed a Gay marriage law *unanimously*. *"Iceland, the only country in the world to have an openly gay head of state, passed a law on Friday allowing same-sex partners to get married in a vote which met with no political resistance."*[100] The Iceland parliament had no difficulty passing the legislation *"with no political resistance."*[101]

In Romans chapter one, the apostle Paul describes a society when they come to the point when God has abandoned them. A few years ago, Dr. John MacArthur gave a sermon on how to pray for our nation. In it, he first detailed the process by which God comes to the point of literally ignoring them, refusing to respond to them, and even giving that society or nation over to themselves so that their *ideal* living situations will become reality for them.

MacArthur points out three steps that show *when* a society has been deserted by God:

1. When a sexual revolution has occurred
2. When that sexual revolution is followed by a homosexual revolution
3. When people's consciences become warped because of their errant thinking, which gives way to sinful and destructive behavior

---

[100] http://www.msnbc.msn.com/id/37638706/ns/world_news-europe/
[101] Ibid

Looking at the first point it is clear that America experienced what is often referred to as the Sexual Revolution of the 1960s. During this period, love was emphasized. Communal living became a way of life, along with sharing mates with others. During the 60s, jealousy was an emotion that was not tolerated well, because everything was based on the concept of *free love*. People were encouraged *not* to enter into lifelong relationships with only one member of the opposite sex. Too old fashioned.

All walls that existed prior to the 1960s that frowned upon and even forbade sexual relations outside of marriage, were set aside in favor of adopting attitudes that encouraged people to *pursue* that lifestyle now. Hugh Hefner came along with Playboy and his intellectual verve and explained in no uncertain terms, with a boyish grin, how much better life would be once his ideals were adopted.

Others like Helen Gurly Brown, who was the editor-in-chief of *Cosmopolitan* for over thirty years, endorsed much of Hefner's views and incorporated them into her magazine. She also published the book *Sex and the Single Girl: The Unmarried Woman's Guide to Men, Careers, the Apartment, Diet, Fashion, Money and Men.* This book literally opened the door to a revolution for women, the way they viewed themselves and their lives.

Before long, numerous "girlie" magazines came to the fore offering views of women barely clothed that men had never seen before. Prior to this, there was the sensual "pinup" girl that the G.I.s would tape to the wall of their bunkhouse, but that eventually gave way to partial and full nude pictures because of Hefner and others.

Certainly, the Sexual Revolution had roots much further back in history as there have been notorious individuals famous for their sexual proclivities and excesses. Donatien Alphonse François, Marquis de Sade of the mid-1700s was known mainly for the sex-related novels he wrote as well as his particular views on human sexuality. His name gave birth to a term often used today, *sadism*, which refers to the inclusion of pain as part of sexual intercourse.

Because of the advances in the production quality of condoms and the new availability of a variety of contraceptives for women, it became much more acceptable to experiment with sex. This, along with the free love movement that had its beginnings in San Francisco with the hippies of that time, moved society ahead in quantum leaps from where it had been.

Movies also began portraying sex more overtly, as opposed to simply *implying* it as Hollywood had done for years. Less was left to the imagination. Because of these trends, pornography became less illicit and more acceptable. This along with abortion laws that made abortions *legal,* first in the United Kingdom in the late 1960s, and the United States in the mid-1970s ensured that where matters of sex were concerned, they would remain on the front burner of society for decades to come.

Eventually, the homosexual community began looking for its own sexual revolution and so began the movement to overturn laws that prohibited it. Moreover, many proponents of homosexual rights believed that homosexuals should have the legal ability to marry, just as heterosexual couples have had since time immemorial. This began the work of bringing the situation out into the open through legal means in attempts to change public opinion.

A number of states adopted laws that recognized same-sex marriage, Vermont the first, with Massachusetts following. A number of other states followed and in California, the Gay and Lesbian communities were determined to make this happen, but failed twice. This has not stopped their endeavors and it is only a matter of time before a way is found to overturn Proposition 8. It is going through the courts now.

Nonetheless, this country as a whole has seen the sexual revolution and has begun experiencing the *homosexual* revolution. From here, it is one further step downward to reach the level where right thinking and absolute truth are seen as *wrong*, requiring modification in thinking. Once society reaches this level – and it has – unmitigated anger is the normal response to God's truth.

To stand up and offer an opinion today in which homosexuality is said to be *wrong* based on the *biblical* truth, often invites a torrent of hate-filled rhetoric. Ironically, those who come against homosexuality are viewed as "haters" or "hatemongers." This has led to people being arrested in both Canada and the United Kingdom for "hate" speech.

As society reaches this level, they want nothing more than to be free of God's chains and so at that point, He gives them over to their desires. The idea here in Romans 1 is that God literally *tosses* them over to reap the consequences of their thoughts and actions. This, says MacArthur, is a form of God's wrath because they wind up being enslaved to the very thing they believe will free them.

Satanic Strategies

SATANISM
SERIAL KILLERS

Consider the fact that the earth itself as well as the weather surrounding the planet seems to be in a state of violent flux. We have been experiencing earthquakes seemingly as never before, along with droughts, flooding, volcanoes, tsunamis, and tornadic activity.

As I write this, numerous volcano eruptions have just occurred in the country of Ecuador. *"Explosive eruptions shook two huge volcanoes in Central and South America on Friday, forcing thousands of people to flee their homes and disrupting air traffic as ash drifted over major cities.*

"Guatemala's Pacaya volcano started erupting lava and rocks Thursday afternoon, blanketing the country's capital with ash and forcing the closure of the international airport. A television reporter was killed by a shower of burning rocks when he got too close to the volcano, about 15 miles south of Guatemala City."[102] These are becoming the norm throughout the world.

Changes Now and Ahead
Beyond this, on June 7, 2010, it was reported that we can look forward to massive changes in the earth's weather patterns due to the possibility of a coming solar storm. NASA has stated, *"The sun is waking up from a deep slumber, and in the next few years we expect to see much higher levels of solar activity. At the same time, our technological society has developed an unprecedented sensitivity to solar storms. The intersection of these two issues is what we're getting together to discuss. The National Academy of Sciences framed the problem two years ago in a landmark report entitled 'Severe Space Weather Events—Societal and Economic Impacts.' It noted how people of the 21st-century rely on high-tech systems for the basics of daily life. Smart power grids, GPS navigation, air travel, financial services and emergency radio communications can all be knocked out by intense solar activity. A century-class solar storm, the Academy warned, could cause twenty times more economic damage than Hurricane Katrina."*[103]

According to one NASA-related weather site, just in the last few months, as of this writing, unprecedented storms, which left massive flooding in their wake inundated China, Poland, Azerbaijan, India, and various parts of the United States. Tornados seem to be a weekly occurrence throughout the United States. The world has experienced

---

[102] http://www.cbsnews.com/stories/2010/05/29/tech/main6530836.shtml
[103] http://science.nasa.gov/science-news/science-at-nasa/2010/04jun_swef/

landslides in Italy and Northwest Pakistan, as well as volcanoes or earthquakes in South and Central America, Northern Marianas Islaccands, Yasur Volcano on Vanuatu's Tanna Island, two volcanoes in Vanuatu, Gaua and Ambrym and Iceland. There have been swarms of locusts in Eastern Australia, which destroyed crops and there have been droughts in Africa, California's Central Coast (the salad bowl of the world), and the Canadian Prairie.[104] This previous listing only scratches the surface of all the worldwide activity since 2009 through the middle of 2010.

While these events may or may not be related to Satanic activity, we know that Satan was able to kill Job's family with a tornado (cf. Job 1:19). Nonetheless, we can also attribute this to the fact that the Lord prophesied these things in His Olivet Discourse (cf. Matthew 24) and called this period *"the beginning of sorrows."*

The whole point here is that things are *winding* down. It appears that this earth was given only so much time to exist before the Lord will fully destroy this one and make another one for those who will live with Him forever.

People are winding down. In many cases, the world is growing progressively wicked. This should not surprise us since God foretold it through his New Testament writers. Just how bad is bad though?

If we go back only to the time of Jack the Ripper and move forward from that point, we can gain good insight into how serial killers have come of age. In the case of Jack the Ripper, the case was never officially solved, though some believe they have arrived at the solution to the puzzle by putting a real name and face to Jack. Others are not convinced.

---

[104] http://earthobservatory.nasa.gov/NaturalHazards/

In either case though, the facts are plain. Jack the Ripper is said to have killed and partially dismembered five London streetwalkers during the Victorian Era.

As far as America is concerned, our serial killer history really starts with a man named H. H. Holmes. He reportedly confessed to twenty-seven murders in the 1890s. Apparently, it was not for a few decades that the next serial killer happened came along in America. This one became known as the "Axeman of New Orleans," because of how he brought terror to that town during 1918-1919.

According to one author, it was not until the "*post-WWII period that serial murder became rampant in this country.*"[105] The United States has seen its share of serial killers and it would seem that more are on the way. Dr. Deborah Schurman-Kauflin wrote a book titled, *Vulture - Profiling Serial Killers* in which she shares some facts about specific cases that are very difficult for the average person to absorb. Her book "*is the product of studying 67 cases of sadistic rape and homicide. There were 18 serial sadistic rapes and 49 sadistic homicides. Beyond examining the crime scenes of these offenses, I interviewed 17 sadistic serial killers. I also selected eleven of the most brutal sadistic murders that I was hired to profile. This was to simply get a snapshot of who was committing these crimes.*"[106]

Schurman-Kauflin's book highlights a number of categories:

- Those she calls Vultures
    - (Violent Uninhibited Liars Talkers Unfeeling Ruthless Empty)
- Sadist child molesters
- Sadistic homosexuals
- Macho man sadists

---

[105] http://www.carpenoctem.tv/killers/history.html
[106] Dr. Deborah Schurman-Kaulfin *Vulture - Profiling Serial Killers* (Universal Publishers 2005), 20

- Profiling a killer

Sadists

According to Schurman-Kauflin, sadists *"will inflict pain on someone in order to see a terrified victim's reaction...The tears streaming down the victim's face, the terror in the eyes, and the pleading for mercy are reactions that arouse sadists. Tormenting a victim is a way for them to bolster their egos and self worth. Having complete control over a helpless person makes them God-like in their own twisted worlds."*[107]

These types of individuals *relish* what they do. They look forward to their next victim and gaining absolute and total control over them. This is essentially what they live for and it brings them a tremendous amount of pleasure. For these individuals, the greatest sexual release for them comes in their control of others, and the abject terror they are able to instill in their victims.

Now, are these people involved in worshiping Satan? They may or may not be. The real point here though is that what they are *doing* is nothing less than Satanic. It must be remembered that Satan has absolute and unadulterated hatred for all human beings. In fact, he hates every aspect of God's Creation. Because of that, he would love nothing more than to inflict unending pain on every human being.

This is why Satan delights in deceiving people through rock music, or some other avenue. By deceiving them into thinking that he's a great guy, and a wonderful pal, they will end up in very same place that he will spend his eternity; the Lake of Fire. Since Satan knows beyond doubt that this will occur, he wants to take as many of God's creatures with him as possible. This will ensure that as many human beings as possible will suffer in hell with him for all eternity.

---

[107] Dr. Deborah Schurman-Kaulfin *Vulture - Profiling Serial Killers* (Universal Publishers 2005), 8

Schurman-Kauflin relates that like an engineer constantly endeavoring to perfect his craft, the sadist criminal is always looking for new ways to torture people to death. This is something that is constantly on the forefront of their minds. It is like a math problem that they must solve, or an invention that they must improve upon.

Like a growing drug addiction, sadists seem to need to inflict more pain, see more blood and gore, and hear louder screams of agony from their victims each time they commit one of their barbarically cruel crimes. For many of these criminals, their gateway into this type of crime often begins with pornography and/or voyeurism. From there, they often up the ante to include more hardcore pornography including videos. Through *voyeurism*, these criminals become very adept at *stalking* their victims.

Many of these criminals start out very young, often torturing and killing animals, as if it trains them for dealing with human beings later on. Whether or not serial killers worship Satan, or even believe he exists is certainly not the point. The fact that they do what they do to such a horrific level proves that they have been taken over by some being from another dimension. That malevolent being(s) simply acts out its own desires *through* the person. The person becomes the puppet, yet he is so intertwined with the demon(s) that he believes his desires arise from his own inner workings.

However, there certainly have been a number of high-profile serial killers who, as it turns out, had a connection with the occult. Robert Berdella owned "*a store called Bob's Bazarre Bazaar in Kansas City, Missouri that specialized in novelty items that appealed to those with darker and occult-type taste. Around the neighborhood he was considered odd but was liked and participated in organizing a local community crime watch programs. However, inside his home, it was discovered that Robert 'Bob' Berdella lived in a world dominated by sa-*

domasochistic slavery, murder and barbarous torture."[108] He preyed on homosexual men.

It was not until one individual who had managed to escape the clutches of Berdella told wild stories of torture, rape, and occult literature, that Berdella's crimes came to light. There was no indication of satanic rituals performed *with* or *on* his victims, yet the occult literature was obviously part of his life and worldview.

Serial killers want total control over their victims, from the time of the abduction to their deaths. Serial killer Ted Bundy wanted even *more*, stating that *"he always wanted to build a crematorium so that he could keep his control over the victims past their murders. He wanted the bodies to be obliterated because he wanted to be God."*[109]

The fact that these individuals feel absolutely no remorse for their heinous crimes, and that they fully believe in many cases they *must* do what they do to gain some semblance of happiness shows how twisted and diabolical they have become. Whatever the true motivation within them is, it can be clearly understood to be satanic.

---

[108] http://crime.about.com/od/murder/p/db_berdella.htm
[109] Dr. Deborah Schurman-Kaulfin *Vulture - Profiling Serial Killers* (Universal Publishers 2005), 114

SATANISM
NEW AGE MOVEMENT

We have dealt with the topic of the New Age Movement in previous books, and much has been written on the subject from others. The New Age seems to be Satan's favored mode of creating situations in which people reject the God of the Bible. The reasons are manifold, but suffice it to say that through the New Age Movement, reason and logic is placed on the shelf, replaced instead with emotions and feelings. These become the arbiters of the decision making process for people. In short, it could be summed up with the adage, *"If it feels good, do it!"* While that may appear to be an oversimplification, it really is not. The more the New Age is studied, the more one realizes that being caught up within the movement means a complete denial of God's absolutes when it comes to making decisions.

Reason and Logic

God wants us to use reason and logic, and to test the spirits to determine whether these spirits are from God or Satan. We cannot merely go by how we feel about a situation because our feelings are *corrupt*. Certainly, our logic can often be faulty as well, however, we have a far better chance of making good decisions if we use logic and foresight, based on biblical truth, as opposed to basing our decisions on how a situation might make our head (or our bodies) feel.

Today's New Age Movement has gained quite a foothold in the visible Church, which is something that was not part of the equation in years prior. In my view, the thing that started breaking down the walls between the Visible Church and the New Age Movement began in earnest with the Charismatic Movement. I say this because in many ways, proponents of the Charismatic Movement often made (and still make) their decisions based on an *internal feeling* or *sixth sense*.

When I was involved in the Charismatic Movement, it was very common to hear people excuse their actions or beliefs with the disclaimer, "*I really felt as if God...*" and that is supposed to end all discussion. After all, if God *did* really speak to these people, then who is anyone else to say otherwise?

The problem becomes clear (or *should* at any rate), that people who tend to rely on their emotions to dictate their actions often wind up becoming immersed in groups created by Jim Jones, or other gurus. Because emotions are directing their steps, they are on very sandy ground. There is virtually no foundation and eventually, they toss out the Bible altogether, because they come to believe that the Bible is too small of a book to hold "God." While that is certainly true, this does not mean that the Bible is not God's Word to us, and that we are to live our lives by the truth found *within* it. If we spent all of our lives studying God's Word, do we honestly believe that we would finally come to the end of its truth? Hardly. The more the Bible is studied, the more study is *needed*. God is *infinite* and in many ways, so is the Bible.

God Speaks?
People who go by feeling believe that God is still speaking to people today, just as He did when the Church was originally formed by Jesus Christ through the baptism of the Holy Spirit. While I firmly believe God *directs* the individual steps of His children, He does not necessarily *talk* to us as when we have conversations with other people. God speaks to us through His Word, and if we toss that *aside*, preferring to rely on feelings and emotions, it is like throwing away your cell phone and expecting to hear from your spouse magically, over the airwaves.

Of course, God *is* able to speak to any one of His children; however, to believe that He *must* or to expect it, is to impose our will on God. He does what He does and we are to do what He tells us to do. That includes hiding His Word in our hearts, so that we might not sin against Him and a host of other things that only come through the knowledge of His Word. He directs us through His Word.

The New Age Movement says that God *changes*, that He is different things to different people. The *Bible* says that He is the same yesterday, today, and forever. Who should we believe? The way you answer that question will determine your relationship with God.

New Agism is merely another name for modern day *witchcraft*. It is rife with mysticism, where very few straight answers are given, and people are encouraged to explore ways to find out who God really is...for each person. The idea that one can boldly interpret Scripture to mean that when Jesus said He is the way, the truth, and the life, what He really meant was that *He is the way, the truth, and the life*, is not only arrogant, but highly questionable, not to mention offensive to many people who are not Christians! That is one of the big problems with the New Age Movement. It deigns to offend *no one*. There is room for all, except the narrow-minded Christian who believes that God's Word is fully inspired and says only one thing, or it says nothing.

In the past, New Age proponents often felt that gaining insight that leads to self-actualization could be achieved through drug use. However, that is not necessarily the case today, as the most well known and noted New Age leaders warn against the use of drugs. They emphasize that drug use should not be used, but if it is used, it should be done with great care.

One individual relates a story of a party in which college age and professional people attended. Drugs were in use, including pot and LSD. As the evening wore on, the party atmosphere was interrupted by *"screaming and thrashing, [the] crash of splintered furniture and hysterical crying..."*[110] It turned out to be a young man who *"seemed to have a superhuman strength as he thrashed about on the bed under the muscles of four would-be NFL linemen."*[111]

It turns out that the young man was having a "bad trip" from LSD. *"During his attack, he repeatedly screamed 'I've seen the devil! I've seen the devil!' Although I didn't believe him then (I fancied myself an atheist follower of Ayn Rand in those days), I believe him now. It is likely that he saw something he identified as the devil and it frightened him badly. So much so, that a year later he was still under a psychiatrist's care."*[112]

---

[110] Joseph Carr *The Lucifer Connection* (Huntington House, 1987), 115
[111] Ibid, 116
[112] Ibid, 116

It is very possible that the use of drugs removes any barriers that keep Satan and his cohorts from having a direct connection to the human mind. Drugs take over certain functions of the brain that most are unable to control. Many New Agers believe that because of the current state of a human being's consciousness, we are unable to achieve the knowledge and resultant higher spiritual levels. For this to occur, more is required, a disconnect with our current consciousness which would allow each person to *self-actualize*, or get in touch with their inner divinity.

Various techniques within the New Age are taught to help people achieve that level. Drugs can also accomplish that disconnect. Once the disconnect is made, *anything* can come in to fill the void. These are ways in which people can alter their consciousness. *"Using psychoactive drugs to raise consciousness is as old as man himself. Ever since early man ate the wrong fruit, he has been having such experiences. Drugs are also recognized as among the most dangerous methods, the most crude methods but are also among the most popular methods."*[113]

Of course, it must be remembered that even though New Agers often reference "Lucifer" in their writings, speeches, and discussions, this Lucifer is *not* the Satan of the Bible. He is a version of Satan that has had all of his inherent evil removed from him. He represents the good in man and in this universe, whereas the God of the universe is seen as callous, evil, spiteful, and jealous, not wanting humanity to gain any real insight. This is essentially the lie that Satan through the serpent told Eve in the Garden of Eden and it is still working to ensnare people today.

The New Age Movement has done more to pull people away from God than anything else has done. It is a major tool of Satan because it is so much like a chameleon, always changing, but saying the same

---

[113] Joseph Carr *The Lucifer Connection* (Huntington House, 1987), 117

thing. Conversely, the Bible represents *God*. The Word was *with* God, and the Word *was* God (John 1:1).

People today are given two choices; to believe Satan, or to believe God. God has presented one way of salvation. Satan comes along and has done the same exact thing with the New Age Movement that he did when he tempted our first parents, Adam and Eve. He calls God a liar every time.

Every person who agrees with Satan and follows him down the road labeled New Age Movement, also calls God a liar. The New Age Movement is one of the primary channels Satan constantly uses to get his perspective across to this world, thereby changing society's worldview in stages. He has come a long way in his efforts, and there is much more to come.

SATANISM
Drug & Human Trafficking

As we have mentioned drugs and the drug cartel are big business throughout the world. Once people get hooked on drugs, drug dealers know they often have a customer for life, however short the life of that person may be. Larry Kahaner points out in his book, *Cults That Kill*, that there is often a connection between *"drugs and pornography rings with nationwide connections to occult groups."*[114]

---

[114] Larry Kahaner *Cults That Kill* (Warner Books 1988), vii

In one case, Detective Jim Bradley relates a situation with a person of interest believed to have been part of a group known as *Abaqua*. *"I knew he was a Santero, but I didn't know which sect. I knew he was involved in drugs (cocaine), and that gave us the go ahead. We had some informants make some controlled buys, and we executed a search warrant on his house. He had a cauldron in the middle of the floor full of animal bones, money, human bones, .45 caliber, crucifix, knife, necklaces. He had what I call voodoo dolls, a red one, a white one, and a black one. He had photos on the faces and pins in them. He had a snake in the cauldron, but you couldn't see it easily. I almost put my hand in there."*[115]

In another case with another officer, he indicated how the drug scene is always in a state of flux. *"Now we're seeing new drug dealers from Columbia who are more ruthless than any others I've seen, and I've been on the force for almost ten years, three with narcotics. They are very heavily armed – Uzis, you name it. We find dead bodies of dealers who were killed as part of a drug deal, and they were killed as part of a Santeria sacrifice. All the indicators are there. Sometimes we find small animals, chickens, ducks, whatever, along with the deceased that were sacrificed first.*

"These guys wear necklaces with the color of their Orishas to protect them from the police. They sprinkle powders to keep away the law. One time we showed up late to a drug buy. Everyone was gone but we found dead animals that were sacrificed to ensure that the deal would go all right. This mixing of religion and crime is very dangerous. It gives these guys the feeling that they can't be touched, that they're somehow protected, like they were Superman. It makes them that much more wild and reckless and dangerous."[116]

---

[115] Larry Kahaner *Cults That Kill* (Warner Books 1988), 124
[116] Ibid, 125

As is often the case, those who dabble in certain "beginner" drugs, quickly want something more. Our bodies get used to doses of one thing, and something else is needed. This is often true with prescription medication as well. Our bodies build up a tolerance to one drug and because of that, the efficacy of the drug is lost. In that case, doctors will often prescribe another drug that does the same type of thing, yet slightly differently. This tricks our bodies into thinking that it is receiving something completely new.

Drugs are Not the Only "Traffick"
People who start on cocaine for instance, often need larger and larger doses of it to obtain the same type of high they had previously. The length of time in between fixes is also often shortened due to the body's *response*. Because of the strength of illegal drugs like cocaine, people often become incapacitated or killed because their bodies cannot continue to handle the stress of their physical reaction to the drug, and eventually gives out.

We are well aware of how bad the drug trade has become. The D.A.R.E. program that began in public schools was due to the torture and death of DEA agent Enrique Camarena. He was stationed in a very rough part of Mexico to learn what he could about the drug trade and how it worked there, as well as how it got into this country. With only three weeks to go before he would have been transferred out of his Mexican post back to the United States, he was kidnapped in broad daylight and over a period of 30 hours, tortured and then killed. The drug runners were so vicious that they had a doctor on hand to inject Camarena with drugs so that when he passed out, he would come out of it to experience the hell he was being put through.

There were rumors of the lack of help from the United States government during Camarena's kidnapping, torture, and death. Even before he was kidnapped, many agents felt that their agency and the CIA had all but abandoned them. As it turns out, there were admissions later that government agencies could have done more to protect the men in Mexico, who were virtually on the front lines of the drug wars.

For Camarena's situation, it was later determined that the DEA agents in Mexico, who were essentially on the front lines of the drug war, were left with virtually no back up. Little was done to keep them safe during their assignment in Mexico as the Camarena case shows.

In spite of all that the government has stated and seemingly done, the drug wars continue. Drug trafficking continues virtually unabated and a number of ranchers along the Texas/Mexico border have been killed by illegal immigrants who have pretended to be sick, only to kill the rancher when his guard was down.

The reason for these killings has to do with the fact that drug runners have been using a number of these ranches to transport drugs from Mexico up to the United States. As ranchers discover it, they attempt to stop it, and drug couriers are sent to silence the rancher, and hopefully instill fear in anyone else who would attempt to stop the cartel from using wide-open ranch lands as a throughway to transport drugs to the United States and beyond.

It seems that *if* the authorities really wanted to stop the drug trade, they could do so. However, putting a stop to it means a number of things to the world's elite:

- *Loss of billions in revenue*
- *No drug addicts to control or help to die this reducing the world's population*
- *Possible annihilation of a number of country's economic endeavors with the poppy plant, etc., that would throw those countries into economic turmoil*

Therefore, the drug cartels continue to produce drugs and ship them wherever they can, knowing that every once in a while, some of them might get caught and/or lose their drug stash and cash, but overall, they appear free to do what they do. Much of the trouble in Mexico is between individual drug cartels. It is likely that we will never see a complete stop in the drug trade simply because of the demand for it.

The drug cartels throughout the world do the world's elite a huge favor in a number of ways. People die from their involvement with drugs, on either the *supplier* side, or the *intake* side. "*Mexico's daily El Universal, which began counting drug war executions four years ago, reports that 5,612 people were executed in Mexico's drug war in 2008. This year's deaths more than doubled 2007's total of over 2,700 executions. By El Universal's estimates, about 8,463 drug executions have occurred during the first two years of Mexican President Felipe Calderon's six-year term in office.*"[117] Again, the above figures are related to deaths in *Mexico*. Other sources indicate that in many places throughout the United States, drug-related overdoses leading to death are outnumbering traffic fatalities. If the world's elite wants a decrease in the world's population, they certainly have a good reason *not* to stop drug trafficking.

Both economically and statistically, drug trafficking can be good and is likely great business for the Illuminati. Since it seems clear that they do not live by the Golden Rule, and believe that they are allowed to do anything they can do to keep their hidden knowledge hidden, while bringing their plans for world domination to realization, anything goes.

Trafficking in Humans
Besides drug traffic, there is another huge tragedy occurring throughout the world today. It includes children, men, and women and most people through their own ignorance are completely unaware of its existence.

---

[117] http://narcosphere.narconews.com/notebook/kristin-bricker/2008/12/mexicos-drug-war-death-toll-8463-and-counting

It is called *human trafficking*. This is when human beings kidnap other human beings for the sole purpose of using them as prostitutes. This is nothing less than reprehensible, yet it involves millions of victims. In fact, estimates are as high as 27 million individuals – babies, young children, men and women – are caught up in this satanic web of trafficking solely for monetary gain.[118] These victims are often tricked into going somewhere in response to an employment ad, only to find that they have been set up. Once ensnared, the chances of escape are virtually nil. Fortunately, there are organizations around the world that help get these people out of their situations and back into normal lives. Their stories are tragic and compelling.

"Veronica (not her real name) didn't speak a word of Greek or English and was so scared when she got in our car. For all she knew, we could have been traffickers coming to put her right back into the system.

"As we drove, she studied our every move and stayed as close to the car door as she could get. After we were able to get our translator on the phone to explain who we were, she began to relax her grip on the armrest. She told us she had been trafficked only days before and had been raped and sold for sex repeatedly already. In such a short period of time, she had already experienced so many horrors.

"As we brought Veronica into the shelter, the other survivors were waiting to welcome her, show her around and let her know that it truly is a safe place. She hesitantly followed them around.

"Veronica came with only the clothes on her back ... and six-inch stiletto shoes on her feet, but right now she's safe in our shelter – and she's smiling again."[119]

---

[118] http://www.thea21campaign.org/

[119] http://www.thea21campaign.org/index.php?option=com_content&view=category&layout=blog&id=934&Itemid=310&lang=en

Now are these kidnappings related to Satanism and the worship of him? Certainly not all of them, and there is possibly only a small percentage that are related to Satanism. However, we have already learned that many drug lords use black magic and the occult to obtain more *power*, more *success*, and more *protection*, so why not the ringleaders of the world's oldest profession? It is very possible.

In Our Own Backyard
It is tempting to believe that these things happen only in third world countries, or in places in the far east, but it happens here in the United States. Recently, the *Baltimore Sun* included an article on their Web site, which reported on a man who was using a 12 year-old kidnapped girl for *prostitution*.

"Anne Arundel County police have charged a 42-year-old Glen Burnie man with human trafficking and selling the sexual services of a 12-year-old Washington girl who had been reported missing nearly two weeks ago.

"Derwin Samuel Smith, who lives in an apartment in the first block of McGuirk Drive in Glen Burnie, was ordered jailed Wednesday in lieu of $100,000 bail to await trial.

"Police were involved in the case as part of the Maryland Human Trafficking Task Force. They said the girl was reported missing May 25 from Washington and was believed to be working as a prostitute. County police said they learned Monday that she was at the Knights Inn on Route 198 near the Baltimore-Washington Parkway in Laurel, where she was staying in a room registered for one night to Smith. Acting on a tip, authorities contacted the adolescent girl there. Police retrieved her and arrested Smith when he arrived there about 8 p.m.

"Police said the 12-year-old told them she met Smith in Washington, where he picked her up, took her elsewhere and paid her for sex. Then he began taking her from the Washington area to Atlantic City, N.J., to

work as a prostitute for him, police said. She told police Smith kept the money she made, police said."[120]

Forced into Prostititution

In another case, a woman who already worked as an exotic dancer in a strip club, was forced to prostitute herself. *"The woman said the ordeal in which she was beaten, raped and forced to work as a prostitute inside the Vegas Showgirls strip club near St. Petersburg began Feb. 16, 2009, and lasted 10 days. But she acknowledged under cross-examination that she does not remember the specific dates within those 10 days that certain events happened.*

"Authorities say [the woman] was part of a group led by Kenyatta Cornelous that recruited women to work at Vegas Showgirls strip club near St. Petersburg. Inside the club, the woman says, she was expected to give sex to customers. She also said she was beaten and sexually abused by Dyer and Cornelous to prevent her from escaping."[121]

In other cases, based on the efforts of organizations dedicated to eradicating human trafficking, it is unfortunately reported that the kidnapping of individuals for such purposes has *increased*. *"Police in Italy and across Europe have arrested a group of mainly Nigerian citizens accused of trafficking women for sex, European police agency Europol said.*

"Europol said it and the Italian 'carabinieri' paramilitary police had arrested 34 suspects in Italy as well as in France, Germany, Greece, the Netherlands, Spain and San Marino. Members of the criminal group had also worked with two Italian doctors to organize forced abortions, the Hague-based agency said.

---

[120] http://www.baltimoresun.com/news/maryland/anne-arundel/bs-md-ar-trafficking-arrest-20100609,0,7468759.story
[121] http://www.tampabay.com/news/courts/criminal/witness-in-human-trafficking-sexual-battery-trial-worked-as-exotic-dancer/1101114

"Europol said investigations had focused on groups located in the coastal Marche region of Italy, where victims were held in criminal cells led by 'madames' and had to hand over all their earnings to pay off debt incurred for their journey to Italy. "The victims were subject to continued intimidation and violence, aimed at guaranteeing a daily income and to ensure their compliance," Europol said in a statement.

"After providing victims with counterfeit documents, some were trafficked through the Netherlands and France where they were met and accompanied to Italy by members of the criminal group, while others came by sea or through Turkey and Greece.

"The arrests follow a police bust of a drug trafficking network in April, in which drugs were smuggled from Madrid in Spain to the Italian regions of Piedmont and Marche by using drug 'mules', who were often the women forced into prostitution."[122]

As horrendous as situations just described are, people are hesitant about believing that any of these individuals are used in ritual sacrifices. The evidence is revealing otherwise from a variety of sources. *"Caroline Aya was playing in front of her house in January when a neighbor put a cloth over her mouth and fled with her.*

"A couple of days later, the 8-year-old's body was found a short walk away — with her tongue cut out. Police believe she was offered up as a human sacrifice in a ritual killing, thought to bring wealth or health."[123]

The same article went onto note, *"The practice of human sacrifice is on the rise in Uganda, as measured by ritual killings where body parts, often facial features or genitals, are cut off for use in ceremonies. The number of people killed in ritual murders last year rose to a new high of at least 15 children and 14 adults, up from just three cases in 2007,*

---

[122] http://www.humantrafficking.org/updates/868
[123] http://www.guardian.co.uk/world/feedarticle/9017868

according to police. The informal count is much higher — 154 suspects were arrested last year and 50 taken to court over ritual killings."[124]

Believing the Message in Movies

It appears that these children are sacrificed for the same reason, which is power, and money. "*The rise in human sacrifices in Uganda appears to come from a desire for wealth and a belief that drugs made from human organs can bring riches, according to task force head Moses Binoga. They may be fueled by a spate of **violent Nigerian films that are growing in popularity, and showcase a common story line: A family reaping riches after sacrificing a human**.*"[125] (emphasis added)

Uganda seems unusually hard hit by child kidnappings and resultant sacrificial killings. "*When James Katana returned from a church service to his village in the Bugiri district of eastern Uganda he was told that his three-year old son had been taken away by strangers.*

"'We were looking for my child for hours, but we couldn't find him,' he said. 'Someone rang me and told me my son was dead and had been left in the forest. I ran there and saw him lying in a pool of blood. His genitals had been cut off, but he was still alive.' A witch-doctor is now in police custody, accused of the abduction and attempted murder of the boy."[126]

"*In 2008 more than 300 cases of murder and disappearances linked to ritual ceremonies were reported to the police with 18 cases making it to the courts. There were also several high-profile arrests of parents and relatives accused of selling children for human sacrifice.*"[127]

---

[124] http://www.guardian.co.uk/world/feedarticle/9017868
[125] Ibid
[126] http://www.guardian.co.uk/world/2009/sep/06/uganda-child-sacrifice-ritual-murder
[127] Ibid

There are a number of factors involved in this situation and it may well have to do with economics. *"Looming food shortages and famine hitting Uganda's poorest in the north and east are also feeding the demand for sacrificial rituals. 'These are not poor people paying for these rituals, they are the wealthy elite taking advantage of the desperate poor,' said Binoga. 'In January a 21-year-old woman was jailed for 16 months for kidnapping a child and trying to sell him to a witch-doctor for a large sum. These cases are on the increase'."*[128]

Because of the many incidents occurring within Uganda, it has become known as a central hub for this type of crime because of the epic proportions of the problem. Law enforcement is trying very diligently to eliminate the problem, but because of economics and superstitions, it is difficult for people to stop the activity of selling their children. This is certainly no excuse, but it is how people are learning to think in order to survive.

India's Bloody Ritual
Of course, Uganda is not the only nation that has problems with sacrifices to the gods. In 2009, it was reported that in Nepal, *"The ceremony began with prayers in a temple by tens of thousands of Hindus before dawn Tuesday. Then it shifted to a nearby corral, where in the cold morning mist, scores of butchers wielding curved swords began slaughtering buffalo calves by hacking off their heads.*

"Over two days, 200,000 buffalo, goats, chickens and pigeons will be killed as part of a blood-soaked festival held every five years to honor Gadhimai, a Hindu goddess of power."[129]

So in order to appease Gadhimai, over 200,000 animals were killed, animals that could have been used to feed the starving in India. The

---

[128] http://www.guardian.co.uk/world/2009/sep/06/uganda-child-sacrifice-ritual-murder
[129] http://www.huffingtonpost.com/2009/11/24/gadhimai-festival-photos_n_369446.html

lack of logic in this entire situation screams out. *"Many Nepalis believe that sacrifices in Gadhimai's honor will bring them prosperity. They also believe that by eating the meat, which is taken back to their villages and consumed during feasts, they will be protected from evil."*

On one hand, they sacrifice animals in order to gain *prosperity*, yet they are killing the very animals that *could* provide that prosperity (or at least food!) all because they believe that some god will bless them. The photos that were included in the article were gruesome.

Back in Africa, there are other countries where ritual sacrifices are used. In the latter part of 2009, an article was published on a Web site that highlighted these types of occurrences. *"There was a slight chill to the early autumn air as IT consultant Alan Minter hurried across Tower Bridge on his way to a meeting. Something bobbing around in the Thames below caught his eye and distracted him. At first he thought the brown, spherical object was a beer keg that had fallen off one of the disco boats. But then he realized it was something far more sinister – a tiny, headless and limbless human body."*[130]

The perpetrators of these crimes seem to be absolutely heartless and in reality they are that. The difficulty though is that to *them*, they are simply doing something that will give them an edge. In this particular case, it was determined that the boy was between four to eight years of age, black and most likely from the *"Benin City area of Nigeria, in West Africa"*[131] The police gave him the name "Adam."

The most horrific part of the child's ordeal was how he died. *"Adam had been poisoned 48 hours before his death with the Calabar bean, a West African trailing vine, which would have left him paralyzed but conscious while his throat was cut"*[132]

---

[130] http://www.doktorsnake.com/2009/11/10/human-sacrifice/
[131] Ibid
[132] Ibid

The tragedy here is that these sacrifices are born of the highest form of selfishness. A number of years before "Adam's" murder, another baby girl had been found in virtually the same condition. It was learned later that the father of the girl believe that by ritually killing her as he did, he would bring *himself* good luck.

It's Juju

It was natural then to wonder if this was the same reason that someone had killed Adam in such a fashion. *"The idea that this fate may also have befallen Adam was apparently confirmed when Scotland Yard detectives were contacted by Colonel Kobus Jonker, the retired head and founder of the South African Police Service's occult unit, and a crusading born-again Christian who had made it his life's work to fight Satanic and occult crime. He told them that around 300 ritual slayings, often of children, occur every year in his country.*

"A similar number occur annually in Nigeria, he said, where the sacrificial victim's blood is offered to the gods, spirits or ancestors – usually in the hope that these spiritual entities will deliver riches or power in return.

"In Jonker's opinion Adam had fallen victim to practitioners of the dark side of Juju[133]*, a generic term for African paganism and magic.*

"Being completely unfamiliar with the occult as a motive for murder, British police went on a research trip to Africa, where they spoke to witchdoctors and shamans, as well as to special occult police units. They later took the investigation to Adam's home area, around Benin City, and gradually pieced together a terrifying tale of ritual murder, child trafficking and witchcraft cults that stretched all the way from Africa to London."[134] (emphasis added)

---

[133] Juju was discussed in a previous work by the author titled *Spiritual Terrorism*.
[134] http://www.doktorsnake.com/2009/11/10/human-sacrifice/

While this type of medieval, superstitious behavior shocks us, people who are familiar with it seem not to bat an eye. The article indicated that a witch doctor had stated that animal as well as human sacrifices had gone on for years. It was simply accepted as part of the cultural norm. The author of the article then refers to Mark Kilroy, whom we have already discussed, and Cuban-American cult leader, Adolfo De Jesus Constanzo. The article went onto indicate that, *"Constanzo's obsession with the nefarious side of the occult had led to him performing blood-thirsty rituals that included torturing and sodomizing his victims, along with ripping out their organs. Human and animal parts were then boiled in a cauldron over which magical rites were performed."*[135]

If people are not killed as a direct offering to a god, their body parts are often sold and used as talisman. *"In Africa, people (usually children) are all-too-often killed for their body parts, which are used in the creation of magical charms and talismans. Believers in the darkside of Juju witchcraft say human body parts increase the efficacy of spells. A girl's vagina is said to bring productivity to a business, the logic being that females are productive because they bear children. Testicles are used for enhancing sexual potency and performance, while human skulls are supposed to ensure commercial success."*[136]

At one point, the article states that the people who do these things and incorporate voodoo practices in their lifestyles are not necessarily bad apples. People generally involve themselves in these areas of superstitious religious practice because they believe that it will provide *them* with greater knowledge about the mysteries of life. It should be noted that not all people involved in these types of religions take it to the extreme like Constanzo. The problem is that *because* these black arts are becoming more widely known and accepted as attempting to please various gods, there should be a ques-

---

[135] http://www.doktorsnake.com/2009/11/10/human-sacrifice/
[136] Ibid

tion at the very beginning. There are no questions because of how steeply embedded into the culture are these types of rites.

Of course, not everyone uses human beings as the source of the sacrifice either. The problem though is that Satanism in any form is a form of worship of him. This is what people need to be saved *from* in order that they will realize to whom they have been giving their allegiance. Because of the sacrifice of Jesus Christ and His shed blood, there is no need to come to God with any form of animal or human sacrifice. It is done, finished.

How High Does It Go?
Unfortunately, this entire subject of human sacrifices or prostitution is not relegated to third world countries either. In many cases, the trails can often lead to some of the elite of the world. In others, those involved in Satanism may be found in the law enforcement field as police officers, sworn to protect.

One investigator in Ohio learned from one Satanist that *"There are policemen, members of the cult. Their contribution to the cult would be police checks."*[137]

The investigator asked about child sacrifices and was told that they happen, and for the most part, babies are used, because of their purity. Many of the sacrificial rituals take place in out of the way places, like small homes or cabins in the woods. When asked how they keep people away who might stumble onto them, the investigator was told, *"We have guards. They would be watching for 'breakers.' There are three rings of guards. The first would stop somebody, tell him he's on private property. The second would try to you off. He might take a shot at you, but it would be just to scare you. The third would kill you."*[138]

---

[137] Larry Kahaner *Cults That Kill* (Warner Books 1988), 171
[138] Ibid, 172

In Portugal, there have been a number of instances of child kidnappings that may in fact, point to the collusion of the Portugal police. However, it is the innocent parents who suffer through the process and not just by the loss of their child either.

One blogger presents this narrative related to the kidnapping of a little girl named Madeleine Mc Cann. *"While the elite-controlled media have been publishing speculations on Madeleine's case, the author of a blog had predicted that the Portuguese police would declare Gerry and Kate Mc Cann 'arguidos' [suspects] as a tactic to conceal the implication of police officers in the abduction and disappearance of Madeleine on May 3, 2007.*

"In the blog titled 'master of fate' some unusual and suspicious photographs show Gerry and Kate Mc Cann being closely watched by a policeman shortly before Madeleine vanished. The author of the blog who goes by the anonymous 'Inu Yasha' assures his audience that 'the Portuguese police have not really being looking for Maddie because they know where she is. The police have instead dedicated to create a hostile environment against her parents so they can charge them with the dead of their daughter.' Mr. 'Yasha' further continues by stating that 'instead of looking for the little girl since they know where she is, the Portuguese police have been preparing the terrain by working very intensively on creating a favorable public opinion with the end in mind to imprison both parents and close the case'."[139]

For those who are not aware, three year-old Madeleine McCann is a child who was abducted without a trace while she and her family were on holiday from England. Since her disappearance, the light was immediately shined on her parents and Madeleine has not been located.

---

[139] http://the-elite-and-child-abduction.blogspot.com/2010/01/this-earlier-writing-has-now-become.html

This Mr. Yasha also believes that these same police officers may have done this with another child. *"The mother of another little girl who was also abducted and disappeared not far from Praia da Luz, was convicted without evidence after suffering great torture."*[140] The article goes onto say that even in spite of the complete lack of evidence that the mother killed the daughter, or even that the daughter was actually killed, the mother was convicted.

The blogger of the Web site we have been quoting believes that there is a history of corruption and pedophilia within the ranks of upper echelon officials and polices officers. These individuals may well be the culprits in the case.

Belgium's Nightmare of the 90s
Alex Jones is another individual who has been seriously digging into this entire area. According to his research, there was a huge child-abduction and pedophile ring in Belgium that had many officials initially denying it.

Related to this story is the testimony of a woman who claims to have spent years in the throes of this network. *"[Regina Louf] told investigators how, from her earliest childhood, she'd been used in a paedophile (sic) ring. This had included her grandmother, her parents and a pimp - Tony. She now says 'It was big business - blackmail - there was a lot of money involved." She knew, she said, that sessions were secretly filmed without the clients' knowledge.'*[141] Louf was the first of a total of eleven individuals who came forward with these types of claims, all related to the Belgium system of pedophiles. Louf spoke of parties (she also referred to them as "sessions"), where many high-ranking officials, politicians, and judges took part in these parties. She also stated, *'The sessions not only involved sex, they included sadism, tor-*

---

[140] http://the-elite-and-child-abduction.blogspot.com/2010/01/this-earlier-writing-has-now-become.html
[141] http://news.bbc.co.uk/2/hi/programmes/correspondent_europe/1962244.stm

ture and murder; and again, she described in detail, the place, the victims and how they were killed'."[142] Most of these sessions took place in 1996 and among the people she named, Marc Dutroux was among them.

However, in Belgium, Louf's credibility and life was ruined, in spite of the fact that certain members of law enforcement were able to verify aspects of her story resulting in the solution to at least one unsolved murder. That did not matter though, because prominent people in Belgium put wheels in motion to not only down play Louf's veracity, but present her as completely *insane.*

Dutroux, as it turns out, had kept two young girls in his basement for over a year. Kidnapped by *"Michel Lelievre, a drug addict and petty thief, [he] told police soon after his arrest that the girls were kidnapped to order, for someone else."*[143] Dutroux's wife was also charged as an accomplice. The girls eventually died and were buried in shallow graves in Dutroux's garden.

The real culprit to these crimes was discovered to be *"Jean Michel Nihoul, a Brussels businessman and nightclub owner."*[144] Because of his contacts and knowledge of the people who used Nihoul's services, he believed that he would never be brought to trial. Since this has come to light, nearly 20 people connected with Dutroux have been killed, or died under suspicious circumstances. There also appears to have been the possibility of a complete cover-up by Belgium authorities. Hair samples were never analyzed, and a network of pedophiles was outright denied, therefore *never* investigated.

In so many cases like this, evidence seems to point right to the top, the upper echelon of society. This of course is not to say that all of the elite think and act like this, wanting to rape and abuse children.

---

[142] http://news.bbc.co.uk/2/hi/programmes/correspondent_europe/1962244.stm
[143] http://news.bbc.co.uk/2/hi/programmes/correspondent_europe/1962263.stm
[144] Ibid

However, it *is* to say that the elite enjoy a privileged status, one that is normally far out of reach of law enforcement.

Marc Dutroux was convicted and sentenced to thirteen years in jail. For reasons unknown, he spent only three of those years in jail and was released to the public. Prison officials were at a loss simply because it was clear to them that the man was a *"perverse psychopath, an explosive mix. He was an evident danger to society."*[145] If this was the case, why would he be let out of prison and why would the person who made the decision to release him from prison received what seemed to be a solid pat on the back? *"Justice Minister Melchior Wathelet, was rewarded with a prestigious appointment to serve as a judge at the European Court of Justice at The Hague."*[146]

Could it very well be that at least *some* of these pedophile networks *do* go all the way to the top? What other reason might Wathelet, or anyone for that matter, have for releasing Dutroux long before his sentence had been fully served?

It should also be noted that according to law enforcement, not long after Dutroux's release, little girls in Dutroux's neighborhood began disappearing. In spite of this, the local police did not seem to be able to put two and two together where Dutroux is concerned.

Eventually, Dutroux was arrested because the claims by some (including Dutroux's own mother) were finally given ear. *"Two days after the arrests, police again searched Dutroux's home and discovered the soundproof dungeon/torture center. As CNN reported, three years earlier 'police ignored tips from an informant who said Dutroux was building secret cellars to hold girls before selling them abroad.' In addition, in 1995, the same informant had told police that Dutroux had offered an unidentified third man 'the equivalent of $3,000 to $5,000 to kidnap girls.' Incredibly, it was later reported by the Guardian that po-*

---

[145] http://www.jesus-is-savior.com/Evils%20in%20America/Porno/abuse.htm
[146] Ibid

lice actually had in their possession a videotape of the dungeon being constructed: 'Belgian police could have saved the lives of two children [who were] allegedly murdered by the paedophile Marc Dutroux if they had watched a video seized from his home which showed him building their hidden cell.' The tape had been seized in one of the earlier searches.

"At the time of the final search, two fourteen-year-old girls were found imprisoned in the dungeon, chained and starving. They described to police how they had been used as child prostitutes and in the production of child pornography videos. More than 300 such videos were taken into custody by the police."[147]

Over time, more bodies were discovered in the houses that Dutroux owned. As the body count began to grow, Nihoul "confessed to organizing an 'orgy' at a Belgian chateau that had been attended by government officials, a former European Commissioner, and a number of law enforcement officers. A Belgian senator noted, quite accurately, that such parties were part of a system 'which operates to this day and is used to blackmail the highly placed people who take part'."[148]

This goes back to what David Icke is quoted as saying, regarding a top-ranking Satanist from Australia who on his deathbed explained the process by which high-ranking officials were caught in a web of deceit and blackmail through pedophilia. As they participated in these and other orgies, they were filmed or photographed. That evidence would be used against them if the organizers did not get what they wanted from them.

Franklin Cover Up

Who is not aware of the Franklin Cover-up, in which Lawrence King purportedly stole millions of dollars from a security and loan business he established for the community in which he was associated?

---

[147] http://www.jesus-is-savior.com/Evils%20in%20America/Porno/abuse.htm
[148] Ibid

Often presented as a conservative Republican and a patriot, he gave speeches at a Republican Convention and even sang the National Anthem. Yet, in spite of this outward display of loyalty to the United States and the values upon which this country was founded, there was something terribly dreadful going on behind the scenes. As it turns out, King and an accomplice, Craig Spence had set up a secretive pedophile ring.

There were other networks as well; one other group referred to as "The Finders" created such network prior to King. Apparently, this group was involved in kidnapping children, using them in rituals, and brainwashing them as well. The group of about 40 individuals – allegedly led by a man named Marion Pettie – turned out to be a well-oiled machine which provided kidnapped children to various parts of the world. Once the group had been discovered by law enforcement and their known premises raided, a good deal of information was uncovered.

Author David McGowan (from which these quotes were taken), noted in his five part article titled, *"The Pedophocracy: Finders Keepers"* that in one case, *"inspection of the premises disclosed numerous files relating to activities of the organization in different parts of the world. Locations [he] observed are as follows: London, Germany, the Bahamas, Japan, Hong Kong, Malaysia, Africa, Costa Rica, and 'Europe.'*

"There was also a file identified as 'Palestinian.' Other files were identified by member name or 'project' name. The projects appearing to be operated for commercial purposes under front names for the Finders. There was one file entitled 'Pentagon Break-In,' and others referring to members operating in foreign countries. Not observed by me but related by an MPD officer were intelligence files on private families not related to the Finders.

"The process undertaken appears to be have been a systematic response to local newspaper advertisements for babysitters, tutors, etc. A

member of the Finders would respond and gather as much information as possible about the habits, identity, occupation, etc., of the family. The use to which this information was to be put is still unknown.

"There was also a large amount of data collected on various child care organizations. The warehouse contained a large library, two kitchens, a sauna, hot-tub, and a 'video room.' The video room seemed to be set up as an indoctrination center.

"It also appeared that the organization had the capability to produce its own videos. There were what appeared to be training areas for children and what appeared to be an altar set up in a residential area of the warehouse. Many jars of urine and feces were located in this area."[149]

McGowan ends his article by pointing out that, according to researcher Arlene Tyner (who spent many hours interviewing victims of alleged mind-control techniques), children *"were turned over to military/CIA doctors by pedophile fathers or other sexually abusive relatives. CIA officials also blackmailed family members known to produce 'kiddie porn' in order to gain control of their already abused and psychologically fragmented children."*[150]

McGowan himself believes that it is a distinct possibility. Moreover, he muses that, *"One thing can be stated with certainty about the thousands of victims of today's child pornography and child prostitution rings: some day, many of them will come forward to tell harrowing stories of their early childhood abuse. They will speak of acts of depravity committed against children that are so heinous as to be almost beyond human comprehension. And yet, as difficult as their stories will be to*

---

[149] http://www.the7thfire.com/Politics%20and%20History/Pedophocracy/child_sexual_abuse_and_the_CIA.htm

[150] http://www.the7thfire.com/Politics%20and%20History/Pedophocracy/child_sexual_abuse_and_the_CIA.htm

believe, they will be documented by the images stored in Interpol's computers, and in the U.S. Justice Department's computers."[151]

McGowan wrote this series of articles back in 2001. It seems clear that since that time, Satan has gained much more of a foothold in the minds of depraved people throughout the world. Even if victims come forward, one might imagine them being humored and not taken seriously. We went through it with the McMartin Preschool case and others. It is natural then to ask as McGowan does that if they do come forward, *"how many of these victims will be believed?"*[152]

McGowan's article includes 183 quoted sources, nine references, as well as other pertinent information.

---

[151] http://www.the7thfire.com/Politics%20and%20History/Pedophocracy/child_sexual_abuse_and_the_CIA.htm

[152] Ibid

SATANISM
Mind Control

"Only the small secrets need to be protected. The big ones are kept secret by public incredulity." – Marshall McCluhan

I know, I know. At least some of these chapters read like plots right out of numerous science fiction shows. In fact, considering all the movies and TV shows that have been made, one would think that greater numbers of people now believe some of these scenarios only due to the proliferation of these types of shows. In fact, the opposite may be true. It may well be that Hollywood is doing its best to *downplay* much of this by creating shows and movies based on conspiracy theories that have become embedded in our society.

Biological Weapons?

Recently, it was reported by *The European Union Times*, that the U.S. is testing biological weaponry on its own citizens. The article stated, *"is using its citizens as guinea pigs to test biological weapons and simulate germ warfare attacks in different locations across the country."*[153]

The difficulty of course, is ever being able to *prove* such charges. It is not difficult for most people to now believe for instance, that the U.S. government has covered up the UFO situation for years. However, it has still not been proven beyond doubt that this is the case.

So it is with every conspiracy theory that is bandied about. The oneness is on the person or persons making the claims. At most, we have circumstantial evidence and at times, precious little of that.

Still, there are some good reasons to believe that this in fact, may be occurring throughout the United States. The article goes onto say, "'*According to Dr. Hanley Watson, a former military scientist, the US Army, 'from 1950 to at least mid-1976' conducted 'numerous experiments simulating biological or germ warfare attacks in dozens of locations across the country'.*"[154]

Moreover, the article states that the Pentagon has admitted involvement in some of these scenarios, but also insists, "*...no clue had been found relating the experiments to the spread of infectious diseases or deaths.*"[155] You have to appreciate the verbiage used with the phrase "no clue." They did not say "no link" had been found, but said "no clue." There is a huge difference in meaning, or could be.

In spite of the Pentagon's *official* position, the article relates "*The biological tests included a 1950 operation off the coast of San Francisco; a 1966 biological warfare experiment in Manhattan in which 'the vulne-*

---

[153] http://www.eutimes.net/2010/06/us-tests-bio-weapons-on-citizens/
[154] Ibid
[155] Ibid

rability of the New York subway system was tested'; and at least three tests conducted in Pennsylvania, Fort McClellan, Alabama, and California with 'fungal substances' to 'perform field evaluations to determine vulnerability to enemy biological attack.' Moreover, the 1952 Alabama experiments caused a hike in the spread of pneumonia cases in the surrounding neighborhoods."[156]

Regardless what the government says, there are facts that cannot be disputed. Most are aware that incidents of autism have increased over time, but few are likely aware that it has increased by over *1700%* (that is *not* a misprint), since 1992 to 2008,[157] and no one knows why. Could this increase in percentage have anything to do with biological or chemical experimentation on the people of the United States? Certainly, unless proven otherwise, it remains a possibility.

In 1997, author Jim Keith wrote a book called *Mind Control, World Control*. Adjacent to the table of contents are two images. The top image is the cover sheet of a Defense Intelligence Agency brief on "Psychotronic Warfare Spiritual Access," and the bottom image showed the X-ray of a brain with some type of implant.

Mind Control?
Keith's book is filled with shocking statements such as *"in the 20th century, scientists in the pay of governments and other monied interests have made technical breakthroughs that render actual mind control feasible, and on a nigh-universal scale. Invasive control techniques have been fine-tuned to the point where the controllers are literally able to get inside our heads and to command us."*[158] While these statements might seem to be taken from some Sci-Fi movie script, there is really nothing there that is unbelievable. In fact, with the

---

[156] http://www.eutimes.net/2010/06/us-tests-bio-weapons-on-citizens/
[157] http://www.fightingautism.org/idea/autism.php
[158] Jim Keith *Mind Control, World Control* (Adventures Unlimited Press 1997), 9

way leaders and countries have interacted with or against other leaders and countries, it is obvious that for centuries, it is always based on a one-upmanship, or the power to *overcome* the perceived enemy. Because of this mindset, it is *entirely* likely that eventually, scientists would delve into the possibility of mind control, all of it related to the coming New World Order (NWO).

It is helpful to understand that there have always been individuals who wanted to rule the world. They are included in every generation, and while some of their never get too far in their pursuit, others seem to nearly make it all the way. These individuals are always present in society and always marching to a different drummer.

While to the outsider, it may appear they want power for the sake of having it, it is *more* than that. They want to be able to *control* people. This is true of the wealthy elite, to the dictators of this world. Ultimately, the ability to control people ensures a number of things:

- *A populace that willingly and without question obeys*
- *A populace that will live in "peace"*
- *People who give up their will, adopting another's*
- *People who are subordinate through control are also predictable*

In the end, controlling people is another way of creating a society of automatons. These individuals pose no threat to society and therefore no threat to the leaders. There is a great deal to be gained by the leaders who can control people. Of course, it is also important to realize that control can only come after certain things are instituted throughout society. The concepts of right and wrong must be completely overturned, replaced with something else entirely. This is one of the largest reasons why there has been – and continues to be – such a growing *assault* on Judeo-Christian beliefs, since the morals found within are based on the Bible, viewed to be God's Word to mankind.

Control Must Come from Within

We must understand though that it is not enough to place control *on people*. That type of control can be easily broken. It is no different from placing a person in prison. Why they may *outwardly* go along with the stated rules, inwardly they are likely to be looking for ways to gain the upper hand by escaping, or by controlling outside interests from within the walls of the prison.

Controls that are placed *on* the person can be removed *from* the person. That person does not so easily remove controls that stem from *within* the person. They *first* must become aware that they are actually being controlled in their minds. This is the difficulty because if done correctly, a person who has come under mind control will *never* realize it. They will simply go along with the established order fully believing that they have arrived at their conclusions honestly, from their own particular worldview. Never in a million years would they come to conclude that they are a guinea pig in mind control experimentation in which the will of another was surreptitiously imposed upon them from *within*.

Keith speaks of the turn of the century, just prior to the First World War. This was a time he states that the world's elite (the ones with most of the *capital*), came together to determine how best to protect their own monied interests.

Around this same time, institutions such as the *"Federal Reserve, the FBI, the institution of the federal income tax in the United States, and with the League of Nations, the first stirrings towards a global government. Powerful men were obsessed by the idea of increasing their power and in advancing the technology of control to enable them to do so, and they were burning the midnight oil to turn those dreams into reality.*

"It was the time of meetings held to brainstorm the New World Order in groups like the Round Table, the Coefficients Club, the Fabians, and the Skull and Bones society."[159]

Considering what Keith just told us, it starts to become clear that control rests on the ability to have power over the way people *think*. Actions stem from what people think. Actions must be *predictable* and can only be predictable if proper controls are in place.

Keith takes us back to H. G. Wells, whose book *The Shape of Things to Come*, clearly highlights the steps to the development of the New World Order. He states, *"the actual future battle plans of the controllers jump off the pages with crystal clarity. Here is an unmistakably clear picture of the New World Order, along with a clear statement of its plans."*[160] Though the work is presented in science-fiction form, the credibility of it as an actual plan for the architects who seek a one-world control seems plain.

According to Keith, it would appear that from the beginning, those who have thought to create a one-world order have done so through a variety of means. This new one-world would of course, be fully run by the world's elite. These people entirely believe that the commoners underneath them *should* be controlled and that those of the elite should do the controlling because they are the only ones *capable* of it.

From another book by H. G. Wells, Keith points out six things that will bring about this needed total control. It reads virtually like what is inherent in the New World Order program. Among them are:

- The world's population should submit to the governance of the control group
- A world economic system to be instated in which all nations would participate

---

[159] Jim Keith *Mind Control, World Control* (Adventures Unlimited Press 1997), 9
[160] Ibid, 13

- Replace private, local or national ownership with that of a "world directorate" designed to serve the needs of the populace
- The understanding that controlling the world's population is necessary through biological or chemical means.
- Limited freedoms for the average individual
- The personal life of individuals should be subordinated to this world directorate

In the final analysis, in order to put something like this in place, constitutions and national boundaries of all countries would need to be eradicated. In essence then, the Constitution of the United States of America would literally become *null* and *void*, superseded by the constitution of the world governing institution.

If one studies the world and its history objectively, it becomes quickly clear order that there are many groups that have been created whose goals coincide with that of the New World Order. In order to bring this plan fully about, there needs to be a number of things that help that plan come to fruition.

On one hand, some of these groups have infiltrated the educational system, with its emphasis, or foundation built on Hegelian thought. Put simply, this is the belief that there is *no* value in the individual, but only in the state. All individuals *together* create value because they *are* the state. Of course, the elite are in command of the state, and thereby control all individuals.

In other cases, groups are in charge of *population* control. This can be done through the creation of wars, or through the use of biological chemicals, or other ways as well.

Still other groups oversee *financial* aspects of the world, constantly shifting monies from one place to another. This can be done artificially to create the false impression of a "crash" for example, or it can be done actually in order to support the work of other groups within the Illuminati.

They Have It Covered
Still other groups are in charge of the oversight of all drugs throughout the world, or prostitution rings. Not only are there large amounts of money to be made, but it is another way to control individuals and people in general. Those who become addicted to drugs are at once under the control of those who organize drug trafficking. Drugs also weed out the "weak" or "inferior" through death.

Throughout the world, various secret societies (and our chart at the end of this book is but a *sampling* of all of these groups and what they control), direct virtually every aspect of:

- *War and peace*
- *Drugs*
- *Prostitution*
- *Education*
- *Politics*
- *Mental health*
- *Medicine*
- *Chemical and biological warfare*
- *Eugenics*
- *Crime*
- *Dictators (who rises and who falls)*
- *Major corporations*
- *...and more*

Many people believe that candidates to the Senate, House and even the president *matter*. In truth, they are all the same. With few exceptions, they are all working toward a one-world system in which only the world's elite of elite make all decisions. While it may appear to us that there is a difference between Democrats and Republicans, too often things are carefully crafted behind the scenes to bring forth the previously made decision of these groups.

Hypnosis

In the past, there were claims that the CIA was involved in various hypnosis programs. Keith quotes Dr. George Estabrooks, from Colgate University. *"I can hypnotize a man without his knowledge or consent into committing treason against the United States."*[161] If true, this is certainly cause for alarm.

Taking it even further, according to Keith, Estabrooks believed that he could hypnotize a small army during time of war in the United States that would go beyond their own personal moral code, as well as the military code. One of the stated goals of Estabrooks was to create assassins that would follow the orders given to them during hypnosis who would then be exterminated *after* they had completed their own assignments.

We should also mention Walter Rudolf Hess, of whom Keith states, did brain stimulation research in Zurich in the first part of the 20th century. His research was apparently carried on by Jose Delgado, who *"is the first to specialize in the implantation of electronic devices directly into the brain."*[162] These eventually morphed into "transdermal stimoceivers" that were *"tiny radio broadcasting/receiving units that were buried entirely into the brains of animals and humans carried electrical impulses to the brain, as well as broadcasting the subject's reactions back to a computer."*[163]

All of this opened the door to experimentation on the ability to *manipulate* the individual. If true, we have a strong idea where our government is moving.

---

[161] Jim Keith *Mind Control, World Control* (Adventures Unlimited Press 1997), 117
[162] Ibid, 127
[163] Ibid, 128

Apparently, under the auspices of the CIA in the early 1960s, it had been determined that *"locations essential to providing conditioning and control of animals has been completed."*[164]

Keith points to a number of known victims of this type of manipulation who were routinely placed in mental hospitals after claiming that they had transmitters inserted into their brains. Of course, it goes without saying that attempting to bring this type of secretive work to the fore often puts the victim in situations of great potential harm. If governments were and are involved in this type of research, certainly, they would not want it to get out to the public.

Implant experimentation continued apparently, and *"by 1994, the London Times estimated that in the previous decade there had been 15,000 cases of persons being implanted with electronic brain devices."*[165]

Future Shocks
As Keith explains, one of the ways to gain more control over the populace *willingly* is to provide them with situations that appear to them to be *chaotic,* occurring without noticeable reason. Though they may appear to come about without cause to the average person, those behind the scenes calculatingly devise the events.

One such event he believes was the assassination of American President John F. Kennedy. Keith points out that the decision to kill the president was made by FBI Director J. Edgar Hoover, among others (including Lyndon B. Johnson). Hoover was also a 33rd Degree Mason and apparently, *"the ranking Freemason in Washington, D.C. at the time. According to some, both Johnson and Hoover shared a "mutual*

---

[164] Jim Keith *Mind Control, World Control* (Adventures Unlimited Press 1997), 130
[165] Ibid, 138

fear and hatred for the Kennedys."[166] Now deceased Texas Lawyer David Copeland, reported all of this and more.

Apparently, to cover the trail, a great deal of secrecy and winding paths went into the planning of the Kennedy assassination, involving Permindex, of Switzerland, as well as other specially created organizations. As Keith explains, the details concerning the events leading up to Kennedy's death are multitudinous, including Kennedy's own father Joseph and the British ruling elite. This group made up what was known as "The Conspiracy" that set out to have Kennedy killed. According to Keith and his research, Kennedy was killed because he *crossed the conspiracy*.

Most of the individuals involved at the highest level of the conspiracy to assassinate Kennedy had made huge fortunes during the Prohibition and their illegal bootlegging, including Joseph Kennedy's ties to the liquor industry.

After Kennedy's assassination (which was done by a group from Mexico, made up of seven riflemen, according to Keith), there was an increase in crime by 80%. This was largely due to the fact that few people believed the Warren Report regarding the Kennedy Assassination.

The entire scenario allegedly served two purposes; 1) to eradicate Kennedy because of what he was planning on doing regarding the alcohol industry, and 2) create a controlled chaos, or *future shock*. This led to a decrease in how people felt about their own safety. This set the American people up for *reprogramming*.

There are of course, allegations that Lee Harvey Oswald had been the victim of brain implants during an eleven day stay at a Russian hospital. Since it is fact that Oswald was seen many times in the company of David Ferrie in New Orleans, then it is possible. *"Ferrie was a*

---

[166] Jim Keith *Mind Control, World Control* (Adventures Unlimited Press 1997), 140

CIA contract agent and the high priest of a small religious group called the Apostolic Old Catholic Church of North America that, according to researcher Loren Coleman, engaged in animal sacrifice and the drinking of blood."[167]

Even in the case of Robert Kennedy's assassination by Sirhan Sirhan, there remains the possibility of mind-control. There is also a direct connect between Sirhan and the Rosicrucian Society along with other occult-related material. Keith also notes that *"Sirhan is alleged to have also been acquainted with a member of The Process group (a Scientology offshoot), and to have attended parties at the home of Roman Polanski and Sharon Tate, who also may have been linked to The Process. Robert F. Kennedy dined at the Polanski mansion the day before he was assassinated."*[168]

Did Mark Chapman murder John Lennon as a mind control hit? It is generally known that aspects of the U.S. government did not especially care for Lennon and *"considered Lennon a menace,"*[169] and even going so far as to tap Lennon's phone. There are many in law enforcement as well as the psychology profession who believe Chapman was coerced to kill Lennon through mind control.

Hearing Voices

Many of these people claims to have heard voices that prompted them to do what they did. When that detail is released to the public, everyone shakes their head and knowingly comes to understand that the individual is plain *mad*. The reader may recall David Berkowitz who claimed to hear voices from the neighbor's dog (named Sam).

This may also explain many of the individuals who have claimed to have been abducted by aliens. Could government officials have abducted them instead at least in some cases? Certainly, not all of

---

[167] Jim Keith *Mind Control, World Control* (Adventures Unlimited Press 1997), 147
[168] Ibid, 153
[169] Ibid, 157

them, but a great many of these individuals either worked *for* the government, or were in some branch of the military, and in some cases, were given top secret clearances.

It is interesting to note that in many of these *future shock* situations, the perpetrators wind up simply admitting *guilt*. No trial, and therefore no information comes out. An admission of guilt, a sentencing and that's the end of it, except for those who believe that people like Chapman, Oswald, and Sirhan did not act independently.

Keith includes a small chapter in his book called simply, "Berserkers." These are defined as individuals *"who go crazy and commit murder. A common thread links many of these cases: their belief that they are mind-controlled."*[170]

One of the big problems that the elite of this world faces, is the burgeoning number of people on this globe. They need to cut the numbers way back if they are going to be able to *sustain* their own quality of life. In order to do this, they must have absolute control over the world's population.

Because of this, we will *never* see the abolition of abortion. We will also eventually see the legalization of same-sex marriage. While homosexuals do not procreate, they do *adopt*. Generally speaking, they do not have their own children, or if they do, the number of children is far less than that of heterosexual couples.

Beyond abortion and same-sex unions, we will likely see *euthanasia* or *eugenics* come to the fore. This will be introduced as something that *maintains the dignity of the dying*, and will allow them to choose how and when to die. This concept was built into the movie *Soylent Green*, and in one scene, Edward G. Robinson's character decides to commit suicide and goes to the place where it is done. He is guaranteed thirty minutes, watching idyllic scenes of nature, while enjoying

---

[170] Jim Keith *Mind Control, World Control* (Adventures Unlimited Press 1997), 169

his favorite music. This may become an option for the citizens of this earth in the not-too-distant future.

The reality that should not be missed is that this cannot take place until the powerful elite gains *absolute* power over the whole earth. Once they accomplish this, then these things can be put into place. It is not too far out there to believe that one day – should the Lord tarry – the government of the world will decide how many children each family can have and after they have had their number, sterilization would be required. It has been the case in China for years and they do it simply to control population. It is a pragmatic solution to one of the large problems of the world.

Of course, the powerful, ruling elite and those connected with them would never be under any of these restrictions at all. Their freedoms would never be eradicated or even touched. In fact, the laws of the world would never constrain them because they *would be* the law.

There is also the great possibility that at least some cults or groups within the New Age Movement were possibly created by areas of the government. What better way to control and manipulate people than by teaching them that they are free to create their own reality, when in truth, they are simply coming more and more under the control of ideas and concepts taught and suggested through their involvement with these groups.

Cults and the Death Ray

Keith lists a number of cults that he believes may have been created by the intelligence community:

- *Charles Manson and followers*
- *Symbionese Liberation Army (SLA)*
- *Jim Jones Cult (and Congressman Leo Ryan's death may have been an assassination because of his determination to get to the bottom of mind-control experimentation)*

- *Church of Scientology*
- *The Finder's Group (a international group of child traffickers, we will discuss later in this book)*
- *David Berkowitz*
- *The White Brotherhood*
- *The Renewed Order of the Temple*

Keith also speaks of "Death Rays," which are based on electromagnetic broadcasting. Though in many applications, this technology is allegedly non-lethal, it can easily be made into *lethal* weaponry.

Keith speaks of the fact that the American Embassy in Russia, it was learned, "*was being systematically swept with electromagnetic emissions by the Soviets (who may have created a brand new super weapon based on Nikola Tesla's experimentation, shortly before this occurrence with the embassy).*"[171] Apparently over time, many embassy workers became ill, some of them gravely.

The CIA determined to do more studies on this to find out if electromagnetic radiation could affect how a person acts. They were interested in determining its possible use in brainwashing and mind-control. They were soon able to create a type of electromagnetic *flamethrower* that was capable of inflicting third degree burns on a person from a distance.

There were apparently, also smaller devices that emitted radiation that could be installed in someone's living quarters. It appears that many servicemen were unknowingly used as guinea pigs for this type of experimentation. This harkens back to *Orwell's Big Brother*, in which the government was able to watch each citizen from an implanted electronic device in each person's home or apartment.

Through much research, it has been determined that irradiation from some of these devices can and does cause numerous illness, like can-

---

[171] Jim Keith *Mind Control, World Control* (Adventures Unlimited Press 1997), 202

cer. We are probably all familiar with cancer clusters that have often developed in people where high power lines sit atop tall towers, transmitting electricity from one place to another.

As more research has continued, it has been determined that what is known as radio frequency radiation (RFR) could have the ability to *"stun or kill...over a large area."*[172]

It has also been learned that on at least some occasions, *"Sometimes voices can be heard in the head from the effect of microwave pulse radiation which causes acoustic oscillations in the brain."*[173] Beyond this, experiments with the CNN network concluded that by using this process, hallucinations or images could be sent to the brain from a distance, *wirelessly*.

Our military has already been using electronic mind control weapons that are small enough to be carried in a truck. This microwave technology has opened the door to other areas in which greater expansion of mind control techniques could be employed.

GWEN Towers
There is also such a thing as the GWEN towers (Ground Wave Emergency Network), that are allegedly designed to keep the government up and running in the case of an attack. The problem of course, is that people disagree that this is their purpose. According to Keith, *"the GWEN towers are almost 300 feet tall, and a 330-foot web of copper wiring extends out from them, broadcasting bursts of very low frequency (VLF) messages at 20 minute intervals or, from another source, hour intervals."*[174] The location of the towers can be found on the Internet.

---

[172] Jim Keith *Mind Control, World Control* (Adventures Unlimited Press 1997), 205
[173] Ibid, 207
[174] Ibid, 215

Some sources indicate that the electromagnetic pulse extends to a 300 mile radius and these towers are popping up all over the United States. If these towers are being used for some type of mind control experimentation, then much of the population of the United States would be affected since these towers go from one coast to the other. Many believe that these towers may be one of the sources of contrived UFO abductions and even the control of weather. Could large pulses of electromagnetic current create holograms in the sky? Would they account for why people are seeing UFOs at an unprecedented rate? There is a great deal connected with electromagnetic weaponry, too much to cover in this book. We hope to discuss more about the GWEN towers in another upcoming book.

As far as the subject of mind control is concerned, *if* it exists and *if* it has been and continues to be used by our government, then that coupled with the use of electromagnetic weaponry may also account for at least some of the UFO phenomenon that seems to have come of age. Could it all be one simulation after another? Keith points out that a number of well-known UFO researchers believe that the phenomenon may be nothing more than a cloak to hide the fact that mind control experimentation is being inflicted on the world's population.

As the United States moves rapidly toward Socialism (and will ultimately follow the world toward *Totalitarianism*), one of the areas these groups count on is what they term "controlled chaos," as has been mentioned. They set things in motion that *appear* to the average individual as if part of or all of this world is going out of control. Of course, the reaction to this is *fear* and *stress*.

People want to be protected and they expect their governments to do it. They want to feel safe walking down the street and they anticipate laws to be enacted that will create those feelings of security.

The Problems of 9/11
The 9/11 situation in which the World Trade Towers pancaked to the ground allegedly by Muslim terrorists who hijacked planes and flew them into the buildings caused major fear and anger in the United States. Those planes were a direct hit on our own feelings of security. It reminded us of Pearl Harbor, which was the only other time that foreign invaders attacked us on United States soil.

We had come to believe we were safe from this type of attack. Who would dare to come against the United States? The government told us that terrorists did it. Initially, people's anger boiled to the surface and we wanted nothing more than to see Osama bin Laden hang from the nearest tree. It would be his just desserts for the massacre that he caused when roughly 3,000 people died viciously from those attacks. We *then* saw the attack on the Pentagon, as well as heard about the plane that crashed in Pennsylvania, which was allegedly on its way to either the capitol building, or the White House.

Since then, how often do we hear people say something like, *"Sure, if it will make it safer for me to travel on an airplane, then I don't mind having to go through another machine at the airport"*? Most people do not mind giving up more of their sovereign rights (guaranteed by this nation's Constitution), *if* they can feel safer because of it. For them, the exchange is worth it. They have *less* freedom, but they feel *more* protected.

This is controlled chaos and many people now believe that there are questions that need to be answered. Many of the facts in the 9/11 situation as expressed by our government do not seem to be feasible. If the 9/11 situation was caused by our government, then it would have been done so for a variety of reasons, chief of which was to remove freedom from the people of this land. This is just one more step in securing this country by those who control it so that it can move toward the predefined Socialistic order.

Does anyone really believe that president's are actually *elected* by the people? If this was the case, would we still need to rely on the electorate? We use no electorate for any other election.

Having the electorate in place (along with the media that is also controlled by the world's elite), guarantees that the candidate who is *supposed* to be elected, *will* be elected. Not to take anything away from President Obama, but if we stop to seriously consider his campaign, what he said, how he was presented in the media, his lack of experience both in actual government and in foreign policies, the big question becomes, *was it mass hallucination by the media that caused the frenzy we saw during his campaign?*

The truth of the matter is that if we carefully dissect the promises that President Obama made, to a large degree, all he said was *"Change is coming!"* He never said what *type* of change. He simply repeated that phrase and people grabbed it and it became this nation's mantra, just like *"Yes, we can!"*

Beyond this, in the case of his absolute and unequivocal promise that he would *not* raise taxes, it appears that he will have to do just that. This is to the chagrin and disappointment of many who voted for him believing that he would right all wrongs. They were naïve.

President Obama
President Obama is also believed to have *lied* to major Jewish groups who supported him during his campaign because he gave the impression that he was *for* Israel's security, not against it. Unfortunately, as his decisions, actions, and words have proven, he is not for Israel, but solidly *against* them, in favor of the many Muslim nations that surround her.

We are used to politicians telling us what we want to hear, but President Obama is a case in extremes and the United States is now reaping the results. The reality though is that the "powers that be," the world's elite *decided* who would be the next president and made it come true. They primarily did this through the mainstream media, who did nothing but hype Barack Obama as he was running for president, as if he was the messiah.

The media made him literally look like the savior of the world, or at least the United States. People bought it. They began speaking of him as if he were a type of god, come down to redeem the United States from its miserable existence and brought on by the Bush Administrations.

It is very likely that President Obama is a puppet, as are *most* presidents. They have little decision-making leeway, except that granted to them by the *Illuminati*. I hate to sound like a conspiracy buff, but there are too many things that have taken place in our nation over the decades that seem to point to the fact that an elite group of ultra-rich individuals controls much of the world. They do not plan on stopping until they control *all* aspects of the world. That is their plan, and we are all their pawns.

Was President Obama a practice run for the coming Antichrist? This could certainly very well be the case. Look how easily the media was able to turn him into a messiah. As far as this author is concerned, there is nothing special about President Obama. He seems intelligent enough, and he has an ability to put people at ease with his speeches. The trouble though is that he is *not* intelligent or devious enough to be the coming world dictator.

The elite, who look to the day when they will run the entire world as a corporate body, do *not* consider the fact that they will one day find themselves *subservient* to Antichrist. According to Daniel 11, this man of lawlessness will rise out of that future group of ten world leaders. He will do so by overcoming the others, and will foist his will on them, and ultimately, the world. It is coming, and the elite are not aware of it at all. They fully believe that *they* or their descendents will rule the world as a body. They do not believe that from within his or her own, a final world *dictator* will rise to the surface.

It's Satan's Game...Under God's Control
In spite of what the Illuminati, in all of its various forms believes, Satan is creating his own world order. He allows the elite to believe that *they* are doing that and will have the ultimate pleasure of controlling all the people of this planet. In reality, as the elite lie to us, laying in wait to overcome us with their goals and objectives, Satan is doing the very same thing to them. Though they will gain the upper hand over the masses, unbeknownst to them, Satan will gain the absolute upper hand *over* them, and *through* them, the world.

13

SATANISM
Blaming the Jews

Anti-Semitism is once again growing at an unprecedented rate throughout the world. People like President Ahmadinejad speak plainly of their hatred for Jewish people and for the state of Israel. They promise not to rest until the last Jew is out of the Middle East.

This mind-set has been with humankind since the beginning when God first created the nation of Israel, which was intended for two reasons:

1. To be a light to all nations
2. To fail miserably so that God would be able to bring salvation to the entire world through Jesus Christ

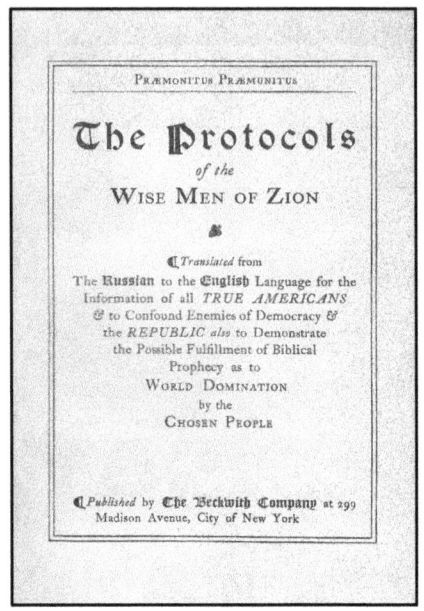

The Protocols of the Elders of Zion

In spite of what people believe about Israel, most of it incorporates some form of *hatred* or *anti-Semitism* toward Jewish people. Mark Dice discusses this in his book on the Illuminati as well. *"For a minority of those who are against the New World Order, the Jews are at the heart of every problem, and at the pinnacles of power. The 'Jewish bankers' and the 'Jews in Hollywood' control it all, they claim. Some still believe that* The Protocols of the Elders of Zion *are authentic Jewish documents that prove the Zionist's sinister plans, and that the Illuminati is controlled by Jews at the very top."*[175]

There are varying opinions about these documents. Some believe they are real, while others believe them to be plagiarized from other documents. One individual states on his Web site referring to the documents and his opinion of them, *"All copies that were known to exist in Russia were destroyed in the Kerensky regime, and under his successors the possession of a copy by anyone in Soviet land was a crime sufficient to ensure the owner's of being shot on sight. The fact is in itself sufficient proof of the genuineness of the Protocols."*[176]

---

[175] Mark Dice *The Illuminati Fact & Fiction* (The Resistance 2009), 25
[176] http://www.biblebelievers.org.au/przion1.htm

It does not really matter for many. It is like attempting to prove that God exists to people who are convinced that He does not. No amount of discussion, debate, or arguing will win the argument. What these people need is to simply have their eyes opened, and of course, they would say the same thing about people who believe the Protocols to be *fraudulent*.

The best that can be hoped for is that by continuing to present evidence that shows the Protocols to be plagiarized, people will *eventually* come around to accept that position. However, even in this, it does not mean that hatred of Jews will stop.

Rabbi Joseph Teluskin states succinctly, "*Thousands, perhaps even tens of thousands, of Jews have died because of this infamous forgery.*"[177]

Still another Web site unequivocally states, "*The Protocols of the Elders of Zion is the most notorious and widely distributed antisemitic publication of modern times. Its lies about Jews, which have been repeatedly discredited, continue to circulate today, especially on the Internet. The individuals and groups who have used the Protocols are all linked by a common purpose: to spread hatred of Jews.*"[178]

Of course, those who firmly believe the Protocols to be authentic normally point to situations and events in history that "proves" the authenticity of the documents. The original documents are traced back to Russia at the turn of the 1900s and allegedly were based on minutes of a meeting held by Jews who had decided to take control of the world.

It was not until 1921 that the *London Times* was able to definitively show the Protocols to be "clumsy plagiarism." "*The Times confirmed that the Protocols had been copied in large part from a* **French politi-**

---

[177] http://ddickerson.igc.org/protocols.html
[178] http://www.ushmm.org/wlc/en/article.php?ModuleId=10007058

cal satire that never mentioned Jews -- *Maurice Joly's Dialogue in Hell Between Machiavelli and Montesquieu (1864). Other investigations revealed that one chapter of a Prussian novel, Hermann Goedsche's Biarritz (1868), also 'inspired' the Protocols."*[179] (emphasis added)

Of course, these Protocols came to the attention of Adolph Hitler, which further fueled Hitler's desire for world domination eradication of the Jewish people. *"In 1935, a Swiss court fined two Nazi leaders for circulating a German-language edition of the Protocols in Berne, Switzerland. The presiding justice at the trial declared the Protocols 'libelous,' 'obvious forgeries,' and 'ridiculous nonsense'."*[180]

Years later, the United States pronounced their verdict, however in spite of these verdicts people *continue* to believe that the Protocols are authentic. *"The U.S. Senate issued a report in 1964 declaring that the Protocols were 'fabricated.' The Senate called the contents of the Protocols 'gibberish' and criticized those who 'peddled' the Protocols for using the same propaganda technique as Hitler."*[181]

The reality it seems is that in spite of any evidence to the contrary, there are many individuals worldwide who firmly believe that the Protocols are what they appear to be. This in turn feeds the fires of anti-Semitism and it is once again becoming a driving force throughout the world.

"The Internet has dramatically increased access to the Protocols. Even though many Web sites expose the Protocols as a fraud, the Internet has made it easy to use the Protocols to spread hatred of Jews. Today, a

---

[179] http://www.ushmm.org/wlc/en/article.php?ModuleId=10007058
[180] Ibid
[181] Ibid

typical Internet search yields several hundred thousand sites that disseminate, sell, or debate the Protocols or expose them as a fraud."[182]

Like anything else, people are often swayed by how they *feel* about a subject, rather than how the actual facts stack up. People also come to the false conclusion that because the Jewish people were *chosen* by God for a special purpose, Jews then see themselves (Jews) as special or superior to the rest of the world. This is hardly true as many Jewish people in Israel since 1948 do not see this as fulfillment of God's plan necessarily, because at best most are Reformed Jews, or holding no particular religious opinion. They see Israel as a political state, not a religious state.

Nonetheless, people have continually misunderstood that because God chose Israel, people see this as God *favoring* Jews. What people fail to realize is that God chose Jews in order to form the nation of Israel for the purpose of extending salvation *through* Israel, to the rest of the world.

While Israel failed miserably to do what they were created to do, God has temporarily set them aside in order to be able to offer salvation through His Son directly to all nations of the world. This is the extent of their being "chosen." God did not choose them because Jews are somehow superior to anyone. He *created* them because they suited His purposes for salvation.

Of course, when Paul speaks of the fact that we owe a debt of gratitude to the Jews because salvation comes from the Jews, he is talking about Jesus Christ, who is and remains Jewish in His humanity. Because Christ is Jewish, the blessing of his lineage through the nation of Israel goes back to Israel as well as the remainder of the world, for those who will place their faith in Him for salvation.

---

[182] http://www.ushmm.org/wlc/en/article.php?ModuleId=10007058

This type of thinking – the belief that the Jews are the source of all problems and have been trying to rule the world for eons – has created all sorts of problems within society and within Christendom as well. We have talked about this problem in previous works, but Replacement Theology stems from the idea that the Church has replaced Israel. It is another way to take the true meaning of the Bible and change it through the use of allegory. In fact, the only way to make the Bible say this *is through* allegory.

This belief in the Protocols has also created numerous groups that are entirely anti-Semitic, believing that whites are the *true* chosen people. This has ultimately led to the constant tension in the Middle East, with those opposed to Jews and Israel's presence believe the Protocols speak the truth, and therefore the Jews must be overthrown.

This situation will continue until the return of Jesus Christ when He will eradicate error, replacing it with truth. Since He *is* truth, He can do nothing less. The lies that have been told repeatedly that the Jews want to control the world and must be overthrown is one of the best lies that Satan has created. The fact that he has been able to keep it going is testament to his power as master deceiver.

Discussing the idea that the Protocols are nothing but a plagiarized, and therefore, fraudulent work is like debating about the existence of God. Regardless of how many things are discussed, debated, and even argued, people will stick with their own opinions unless they are fully convinced otherwise. Even if everyone accepted the Protocols to be what they are – *fake* – hatred of Jews would not stop, or even be curtailed to a great degree.

Satan hates Jews because salvation comes from them. He will do whatever it takes to ensure that the majority of the world also hates them.

14

SATANISM
Islam, Jihad, and Sharia Law

The plain fact of the matter appears to be that *if* the leaders of the free world wanted to, it would not be that difficult to crush the Taliban as well as Islamic Jihadists. The fact that this has not occurred tells us something.

To many, it may be interpreted as simply the government's inability to stay ahead of the game where terrorists are concerned. Those people might think that we are putting up a good fight, but so far, it just has not been enough. This is one way to look at it. Another way is to consider the possibility that the constant threat of Jihad, or terrorist acts that might be perpetrated against America, and on American soil, is a means by which the elite keeps the average person in a constant state of nervousness and fear. As discussed already, the Illuminati are not above using what is called *controlled chaos* to achieve their means.

Controlled Chaos is simply creating situations within society in which people are always fearful, even when they are doing things that should bring relief, happiness, or joy. The constant undertone of tension tends to wear people down after a while. Because of this, people get to a point where they are willing to give up more of their Constitutional rights in order to gain more peace.

This is something we expect our government to do and more and more people today are falling into this category. Because of this, the government's current move to change or even eradicate the second amendment (the right to bear arms) is under strong consideration.

The government's reasoning is that it will be much easier to limit or even erase the power of the terrorist to harm us. This of course, is absolute nonsense, since both terrorists and run of the mill criminals do not routinely go to a gun store to legally purchase weapons.

Most handguns used in crimes are smuggled into the United States from South America, through Mexico. An extremely small percentage of handguns and other weapons used in the commission of crimes are those that have been stolen from an NRA member's or average citizen's home. The government would like us to believe that this is where the preponderance of guns comes from, but it is merely a myth they are foisting on the public.

People who are afraid of guns buy into these lies, but the rest of us know better. Ultimately, by eliminating the average citizen's right to bear arms, the government is able to do what they want to do without fear of citizens literally getting up *in arms*. There will come a time in the United States where people who go against our government will be incarcerated or worse, as "enemies of the state."

Enemies of the state – in the United States – can be executed for *treason*. The government is working all ends against the middle to bring about their New World Order and it is being done at the expense of many freedoms that we have taken for granted over the years.

People are routinely coming to the conclusion that if they put more safeguards into the airport security system, then it will be safer to fly. So, the government via the FAA makes it more difficult for people to get through security, by making the process longer. We have to answer questions, we have to walk through a metal detector, we have to remove most of our clothing, and eventually, we will have to walk through a machine that x-rays our clothes.

This will make the public *feel* far safer, but will it help? Not really, because it is due to the level of training by those running those machines. I have talked to retired FAA Controllers who laugh at the many security tactics in place now. They readily admit that they do no good whatsoever. They are there solely for the feelings of safety that comes from them, *for* the average citizen.

As long as terrorism is a possibility in this country, people will not feel safe. If they do not feel safe, they will continue to look to the government to provide that safety.

Most people do not want to bother to know what's going on behind the scenes. They believe this is why we have intelligence departments. It is their job to ensure the safety and well-being of each American in this country. Sometimes they fail, as in 9/11, but most of the time they win. This is what the average person thinks.

Terrorists who attack this country, or who *threaten* to attack it, create situations in which people's fears often get the best of them. People then turn toward patriotism and feel the need to support our country. This in turn, puts our government on a pedestal so to speak, giving them the "go ahead" by the American people to do whatever is needed to address the situation of terrorism.

Islam is a religion born of hatred, in spite of what many Muslims will tell the world. The average Muslim does not read the Quran and they are not *supposed* to read the Quran. They will readily admit that they cannot understand it; therefore it must be *explained* to them by their clerics. It is for this reason that they do not read it, because they will simply become confused.

This is very reminiscent of Roman Catholicism from the time of its inception (around the late 3rd/early 4th centuries), when the officials of Rome decided that the Bible was way too complex for the average person to read. Because of that, all Bibles were removed from public access. It was an issue of *control*.

People came to rely on their priests to *tell them* what the Bible really said. For the average person to attempt to read it on their own would create a world of problems, said the Roman Catholic Church. It was not long after this that the Dark Ages occurred and they were truly dark. Each reader is encouraged to study that period of history to understand exactly what society became like, once the Bible was removed.

It was not until the Reformation that the Bible once again got to the hands of the individual. For the first time in roughly 1,100 years or so, people now began to study the Bible for themselves. From this, missionary movements and evangelization began, aspects of prophecy were studied, and the Bible was translated into other languages.

Unfortunately, some of the individuals like William Tyndale and others were *executed* by the church for having the impudence to translate God's Word into other languages. This was expressly forbidden by the church and the penalty of death was meted out to those who did not obey.

Today's Islam is very much like this. Couple this with people who are ignorant *and* can quickly become riled up to the point of killing others, and an explosive situation exists. This is the world *today*. How many times have images been shown on the news in which groups of radical Muslims have just killed someone (they term "infidels," or traitors to Islam), and they are involved in chanting "*Allah is great!*" over and over again as *one* voice, like robots?

Groups of extremist Muslims believe that it is their duty to defend Allah and Muhammad against all insults, perceived or real. This means that they have carte blanche to do whatever they need to do in order to avenge the offense directed toward their god or prophet. Often this means death to the infidel and an infidel is anyone who is *not* a Muslim.

The world's elite *allows* this situation to continue because it helps *them* in their cause for world domination. Once they get to that point, they will be able to easily either squash the extreme Islamic worldview, or continue to use it to their advantage. It really depends upon what works best for them.

Islam believes that the messiah is going to come who will be the last messiah this world sees. He will be fully Islamic and will help instate Sharia Law. Sharia Law is the law of the land in the countries that are Islamic. Rarely are actual trials done, because they take too much time and cost too much money.

Sharia Law is based on mob rule in essence. If someone steals a loaf of bread from the market, and is seen by even one person, shouts go out to catch the thief and as the crowd gathers, that thief's hand is chopped off right then and there, with no questions asked.

It truly is mob rule and that is the best way to look at it. Not all crimes are punished with this type of immediacy, but many are done this way. Others take more time when the perpetrator might be brought before the village council of elders, who will then decide the person's fate. They may wait until they have a number of people that need execution so that they can all be killed at the same time, or may take care of the problem right then.

The above two photos should be self-explanatory, but on the left, a person is in the process of being stoned. The head area has been blurred out for obvious reasons. The woman on the left is being buried in *preparation* for stoning. Normally, a circle is made, the victim is buried either waste high, or neck high, and sometimes a sheet or hood is placed over their heads, then the *peaceful* Muslims who are going to stone the person stand outside of the circle and throw stones from there. Of course, the aim and ferocity of the throws determines how long it will take for the victim to die.

In Iran and other Islamic countries, it is very common for young girls who have been raped, to be put to death this way. Their crime? Fornication, in spite of the fact that they were *raped*, which of course means that they were made to unwillingly participate in the act of sexual intercourse. This is also in spite of the fact that they were raped by a man, and virtually *nothing* happens to the man. It is blamed on the girl, who *tempted* the man and he could not contain himself. This is how Sharia Law works in Islamic countries and this in the year 2010. Sharia Law is such that women come out losers in most cases. *"There is a traceable dynamic in Sharia Law that is bound to lead to this barbarity. And unless we abandon these laws we will never be able to emerge from this barbarity. It was a blunder that Muslim jurists included rape in the Hudood section of Sharia Law that deals with murder, bodily harm, apostasy, drinking, defamation, theft, adultery and highway robbery. But anyone who tried to change these laws ended up banging their heads against the wall. Mawdudi, the founding father of modern Political Islam, claims that even if all the world's Muslims together wanted to make the slightest change in these laws, they would not be allowed to do so."*[183]

Not only is this tragic and indecent, but also *criminal* that men should be allowed to treat woman as such, or for that matter, any other person in society. They are not only allowed, but encouraged to take the law into their own hands and mete out punishment as they see fit.

We are coming to a place within society where our president may decide to put martial law into place. If he does, the U.S. Constitution gets set aside, *until* such a time as martial law is rescinded. The problem of course, is that once this country is put into martial law, what possible reason would there be to remove it?

At that point, the president and our U.S. Government becomes a collective dictatorship. A curfew could be put into place and those deciding to ignore it could be jailed. Other punishments could be set in place to act as deterrents so that the rest of the citizenry will conform to the policies set by the government under martial law.

---

[183] http://actgoldengate.blogspot.com/2008/11/shariah-law-shariah-compliant-finance.html

Satanic Strategies

Our government seems to be already preparing for this, with some noting that there are currently over 800 prison camps that are ready to go, but so far have no prisoners in them yet. *"There over 800 prison camps in the United States, all fully operational and ready to receive prisoners. They are all staffed and even surrounded by full-time guards, but they are all empty. These camps are to be operated by FEMA (Federal Emergency Management Agency) should Martial Law need to be implemented in the United States and all it would take is a presidential signature on a proclamation and the attorney general's signature on a warrant to which a list of names is attached."*[184]

One has to wonder if these camps are *not* for what our government would call unruly citizens or traitors to our country, then why do they exist? Obviously, they are not being used to house captured illegal immigrants, because those people are caught and sent home, only to return with better luck next time.

In order to gain control of the entire world, a number of control policies must be in place, albeit secretly at first, until the government is able to wrest all power away from the citizens of the United States.

Satellite image showing just one of over 800 prison camps set to go in the United States.

When the Martial Law order is signed by the then sitting president, the U.S. Constitution is set aside.

Our government effectively becomes a corportae dictatorship, doing as they please, when they please. All this would be in the name of national security.

---

[184] http://www.mindfully.org/Reform/2004/FEMA-Concentration-Camps3sep04.htm

Once this occurs, the leaders of our nation will have done their part to hand the world's elite the entire globe. Other nations are working toward this as well and it *will* become a reality.

While it may be difficult for the reader to comprehend the scope of this, or even to believe it at all, we only need to turn to Scripture to see that it has already been defined for us by God during the time of Daniel.

What is most interesting is that we do have people who do *not* claim to be Christians trying to bring this to fruition. These are atheists, Satanists and others who yearn to do what other dictators and conquerors of the past attempted to do. They want the world on a silver platter and they aim to make that happen.

SATANISM
More to Come

This book was not meant to cover all subjects found herein, in complete detail. No book can really do that. It is hoped that the reader's interest will be piqued to continue the research that was started here.

The author's plan is to *build* from this book, taking a number of subjects and covering those subjects in a much more in-depth way. This is easier to do when only dealing with a few areas of research. In the future, books will be forthcoming on the subject of *drug and human trafficking* and its connection to Satanism. Another subject that is currently under consideration is a comprehensive look into the area of *mind-control* and its alleged connection to the Illuminati.

It appears as though new information comes to the fore on a daily basis and it is difficult to keep abreast of all of it. The goal also concerns always comparing these areas with Scripture. What does the Bible teach? Some topics are self-evident, while others require more of an intense look.

Ultimately, in what the author believes to be the last days of humanity prior to the Tribulation and Christ's return, it is important that authentic Christians make the best use of every opportunity. The directive from Christ that we should go into all the world to preach the gospel has never been rescinded and needs to be fervently *obeyed*.

Wherever Satan rises to destroy God's Church, or purposes to replace them with His own, God moves like through like a standard, saving those who will be saved. God is not mocked. We know that He rules even when it does not *appear* as though He is ruling.

Satan is on borrowed time and he knows it. The only thing he has left is to keep as many people from salvation as possible. Are you one of them? Are you one who may have simply picked up this book because either the cover or topic seemed interesting? There are two roads in this life, but only one of them leads to an eternity *with* God. The other – though it may be presented differently to different people – leads to an eternal separation *from* God.

Now is the day of salvation. You absolutely have no idea how much longer your life on this planet will last. Jesus came and lived a sinless life, willingly giving up that life in order that every person would have a way to come to God. Still, each person is required to make that decision. Will you believe that Jesus is who He said He is? Will you believe that His substitutionary death was done for YOU? Will you, by faith, believe that it is only through faith in His death that salvation comes to you? *"Faith comes by hearing, and hearing by the Word of God,"* (Romans 10:17). You are reading this material and what you are reading is the truth about Jesus Christ. He came, died, and rose again in order to seal the fate of all who are and remain in rebellion to Him.

Those like the thief on the cross, who had their eyes open to the truth of which Jesus Christ *is*, gained salvation. This salvation can never be lost. It is something that God *gives* you and proves it by living *within* you.

You must believe. You must understand that Jesus is God and that He died so that you and I would not have to do so (eternally). Without faith, you cannot please God. You must come to the point of understanding that it is only through faith that you can reach God. It is not done by works (Christ did everything necessary to gain salvation for us). It is not done by *buying* salvation. It is accomplished for each person when they stop trying to gain salvation by their own hand, their own works, and their own effort.

Salvation is *given* to those who believe that Jesus Christ came in the flesh, lived a life of perfection, never once sinning by doing anything contrary to God's will. Jesus then offered Himself as atonement in order that the requirements of the Law would be *fulfilled*. Once He fulfilled the Law by dying as a completely innocent, perfect Person, He rose from the dead three days later because the grave was unable to hold Him.

Satan wants to convince you that he and Jesus are essentially equal, but that he (Satan) has a *better* plan. Satan wants you to believe that he (Satan) is the good guy and that God is the jealous God who doesn't want you to know anything. If you believe Satan, you cannot believe Jesus. If you believe Jesus, you will see the untruths that Satan has been speaking.

What every person needs is to *believe* Jesus Christ by stepping out in faith. This is accomplished by deciding that what Jesus did – lived and died a sinless life – was actually *done*. Once you begin to understand that this is truth, that truth will change you and you will become a different person than you are now.

Jesus wants you to live with Him for all eternity. Satan wants you to live with *him*. The Bible tells us that the Lake of Fire is the final destination of Satan. Unfortunately, all who follow the devil by *believing* him will have the same fate. Do you really want that?

You have to decide right now whether Satan or Jesus is telling the Truth. Satan has done *nothing* for you. History proves that Jesus died, in spite of what some would like to believe about Him (that He never even existed). Satan has done nothing, except *lied*, *deceived*, and *tormented* you with false ideas about heaven and hell.

This is the most important decision you will ever make. You *need* to come to believe that Jesus did it. He made the way available to you to *receive* salvation. By putting the decision about Jesus off, you will have accepted the road to hell by *default*. You are already on it.

Please. Please come to believe that Jesus did what He did for you. If you are having a difficult time believing it, then turn to God and ask as a father of a young boy did, "Lord, I believe, but help my *unbelief!*" (cf. Mark 9:23-24). God will hear you and He will answer you, if you ask Him in sincerity and with the faith that you have. Please, do it *now*.

Satanic Strategies

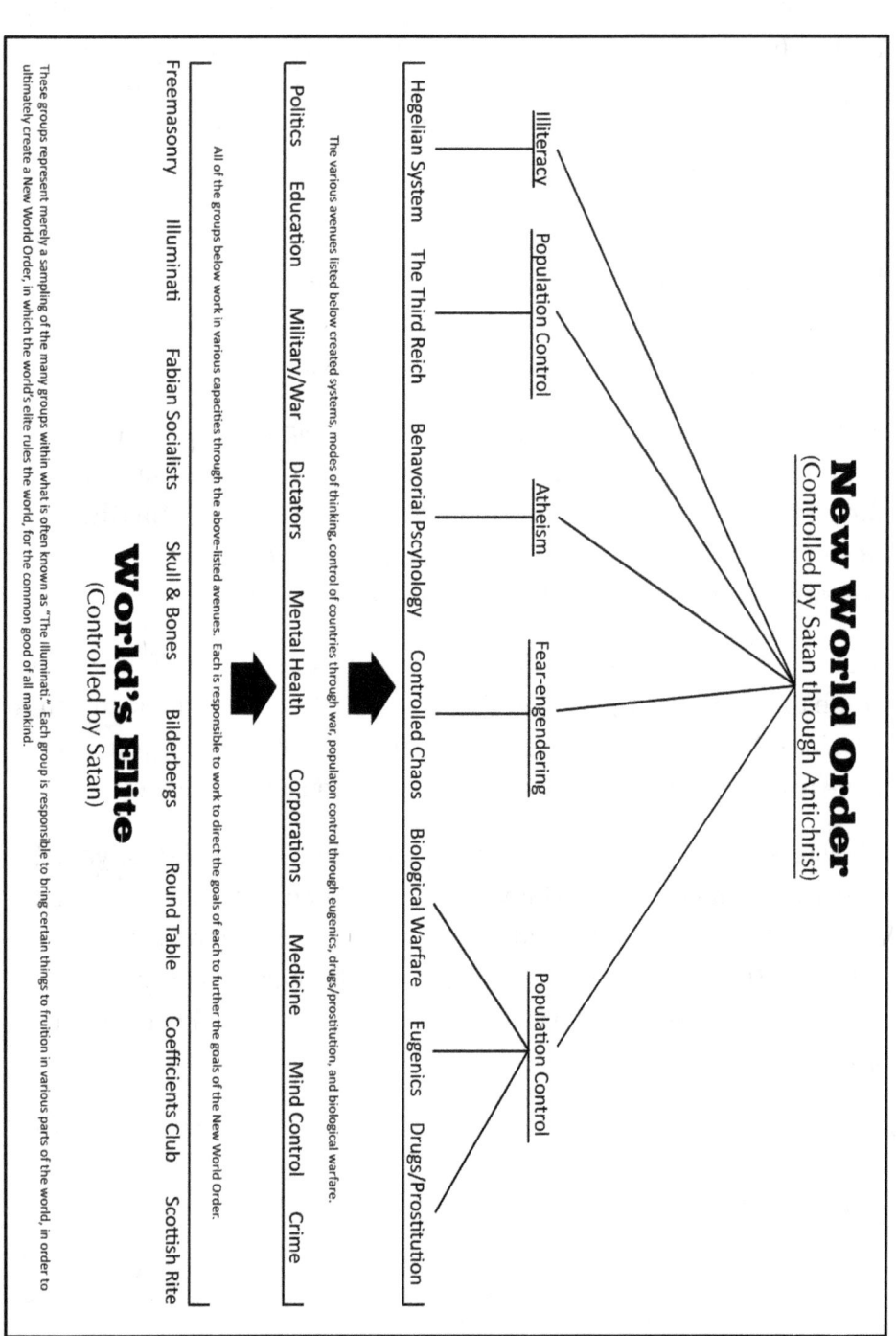

244

Satanic Strategies

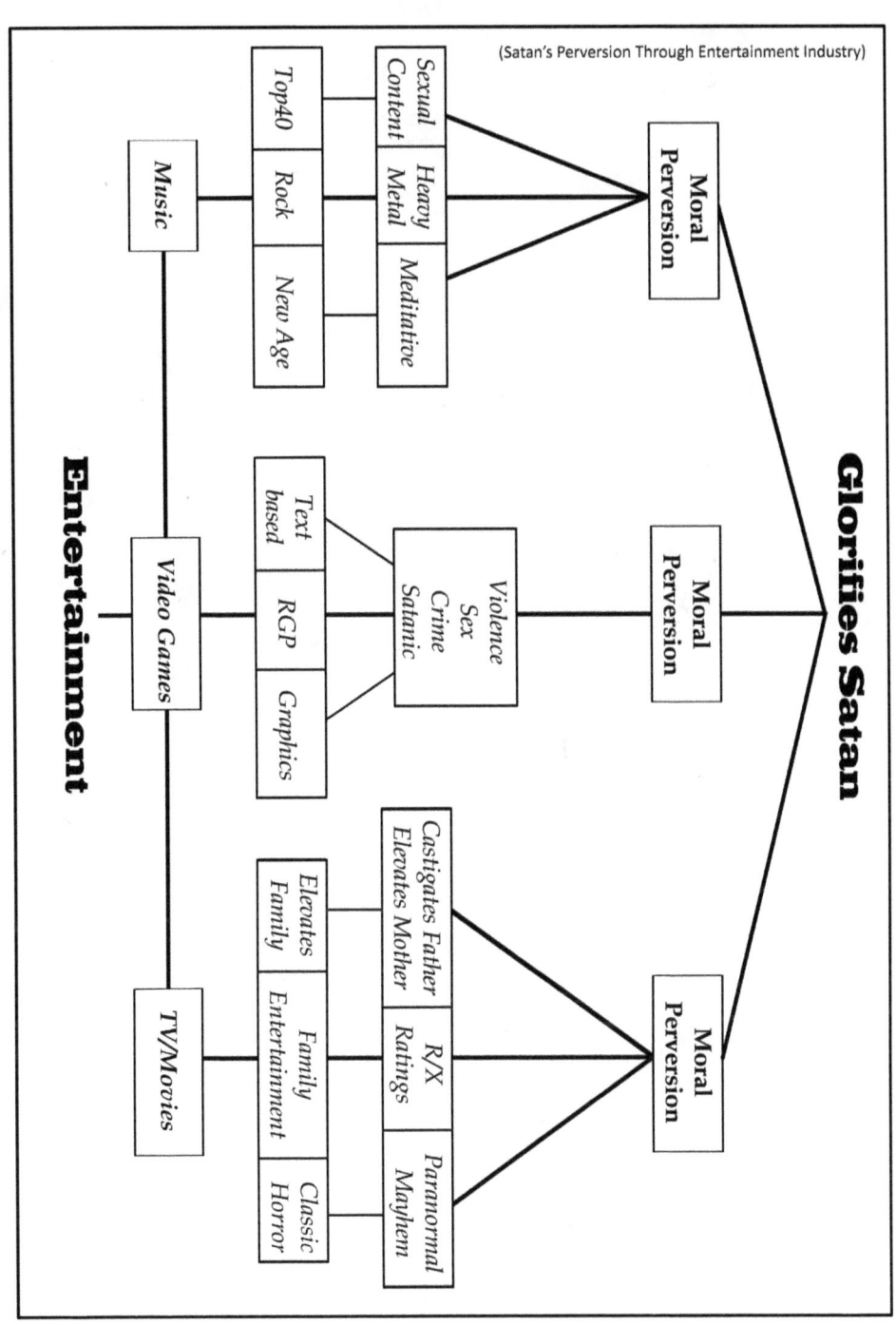

NOTES

Satanic Strategies

Luke 21:28

More Books by Fred DeRuvo

www.studygrowknow.com or wherever quality books are sold!

www.ingramcontent.com/pod-product-compliance
Lightning Source LLC
Chambersburg PA
CBHW080434110426
42743CB00016B/3161